DATE DUE	BORROWER'S NAME	ROOM NUMBER

THE CHILDREN'S ATLAS OF CIVILIZATIONS

25
AUGUSTO DI PRIMA PORTA
MUSEI VATICANI

THE CHILDREN'S ATLAS OF CIVILIZATIONS

TRACE THE RISE AND FALL OF THE WORLD'S GREAT CIVILIZATIONS

ANTONY MASON

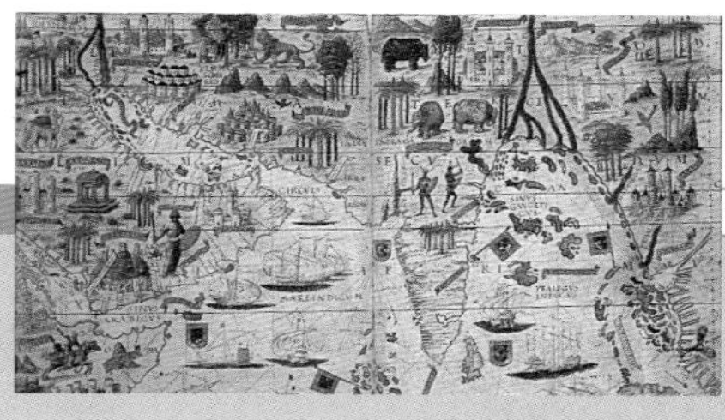

The Millbrook Press
Brookfield, Ct.

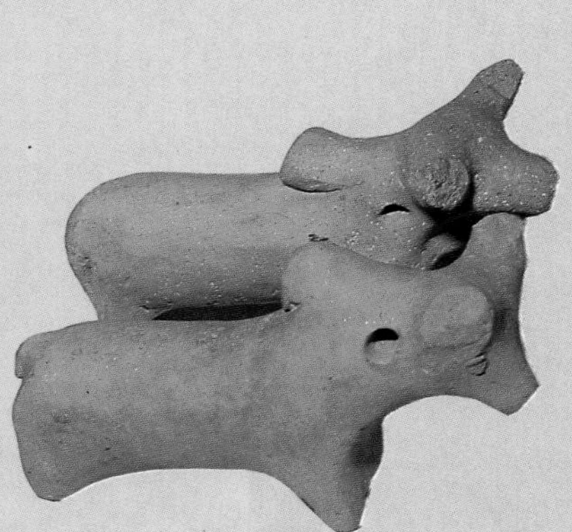

A QUARTO BOOK

First published in the United States of America in 1994 by
The Millbrook Press Inc.
2 Old New Milford Road
Brookfield, Connecticut 06804.

Library of Congress Cataloging-in-Publication Data

Mason, Antony.
The children's atlas of civilizations/by Antony Mason
p. cm.
Includes index.
Summary: An atlas showing the development of civilization from prehistory to the Renaissance
ISBN 1-56294-494-0 (lib. bdg.)
1. Civilization—Juvenile literature. 2. Civilization—Atlases—Juvenile literature. [1. Civilization.] I. Title.
CB69.2.M27 1994
912—dc20 93-23564
CIP
AC

This book was produced by
Quarto Children's Books Ltd
Fitzpatrick Building,
188-194 York Way,
London N7 9QP

Managing Editor: Christine Hatt
Editors: Molly Lodge, Julian Rowe
Design and production: Glynn Pickerill, Mick Hodson
Maps: Janos Marffy
Illustrations: Jim Robins
Picture research: Sarah Risley
Consultant: Dr. Anne Millard

Manufactured by Bright Arts (Pte) Ltd, Singapore
Printed by Star Standard Industries (Pte) Ltd, Singapore
Library binding in USA by Horowitz/Rae Book Manufacturers, Inc.

Contents

SECTION 1: INTRODUCTION

The word "civilization" refers to countries or peoples that have reached a high level of social and cultural development and made achievements in the arts, science, and technology. A civilization is not created overnight; societies take generations to create a civilized environment.

THE MEANING OF CIVILIZATION

The term "civilization" refers to a culture that builds cities, and has all the achievements in arts, science, and technology that go with them. Another essential ingredient of a civilization is the development of reading and writing. The first written form of communication, picture writing, was used over 5,000 years ago. But such achievements are not restricted to city builders, so civilization has a broader meaning as well.

We all have an idea of what we mean by "civilized behavior:" politeness, respect for learning, obedience to the law, and care for the weaker people in society, such as the sick and aged. A civilized society needs stable government and wealth, so that people do not have to spend all their time working to feed and protect themselves. Civilized people need free time to concentrate on the pleasures of life—such as entertainment and celebrations, music, art, sports—and for contemplating the meaning of life itself, in philosophy and religion.

All these elements first came together when early peoples succeeded in farming. Farming villages grew into towns with marketplaces, government buildings, military barracks, temples, theaters and sewage systems. The greatest towns became cities.

Above Grand buildings were the centerpieces of the great cities and the mark of civilization. The remains of Greek and Roman buildings can be seen at Ephesus in modern Turkey.

Right Civilized society depends upon cooperation between all its elements; successful systems of organization are essential. This depiction of the 15th-century Mogul court in India captures the complexity and pleasures of civilized society.

Above Queen Nefertiti was the wife of King Akhenaton, who ruled ancient Egypt from around 1379 to 1362 BC. This bust of her, in painted limestone, dates from around 1355 BC. It is unusual in Egyptian art because it is so realistic: it could represent someone living today. Such images remind us of the continuity between ancient civilizations and our own world—in this case spanning a gap of over 3,000 years.

Right Wealth and power are important ingredients of civilization. By increasing their power over other territories, great civilizations also increased their wealth. Hence many ancient civilizations also had empires. As these empires had to be won and protected by effective armies, military strength was essential. Armies needed the most up-to-date weapons and soldiers totally committed to the empire—even prepared to die for it. Here a military parade demonstrates the power of the Ottoman Empire in the 16th century.

Below The reclining figure of the rain god Chac Mool appears at a number of Toltec and Mayan temple sites. The bold, compact shapes of this statue, and its wealth of jewelry, are typical of Mayan art. The art of some cultures, such as that of ancient Greece, shows realistic images of people and things. Other cultures, such as the Mayan civilization, were far more interested in patterns and shapes. Each civilization had its own uses for art, and its own very distinct traditions.

The world of knowledge

Civilization depends upon a steady accumulation of knowledge—about farming and building techniques, about traditions of religion and art, about astronomy and science. Such knowledge is passed down from generation to generation by myths and stories as well as in schools and libraries.

A single map such as this one, showing a 16th-century view of the Indian Ocean, represents the accumulation of hundreds of observations by navigators, travelers and other mapmakers.

DIGGING UP THE PAST

We know about ancient civilizations from two main sources. First, there are the histories and chronicles—sometimes little more than myths—which were recorded at the time or written down later. Second, there is evidence from the remains of these civilizations. Archaeologists use many techniques to find out how old something is. Older buildings are generally found underneath later ones during excavations, and the different styles of pottery belonging to each age provide further clues to the date of a site.

The ancient cities of the world—from Mesopotamia to Central America—were centers of power and culture where scientists, scholars, and poets met. Here craftsmen produced the beautifully worked jewelry, ornaments, toys, and weapons that modern archaeology has uncovered.

Archaeologists can discover a remarkable amount about ancient cities by careful exploration of their sites—even if only the foundations of the buildings remain. Every artifact that is found helps us to piece together our knowledge of a civilization. Weapons, buildings, jewelry, painting, and sculpture—even pots and pans and farm implements—can all tell us a great deal about how peoples of the past lived and how they viewed the world around them.

Left All ancient people believed strongly in life after death. All kinds of goods were buried with the dead so that they would be able to enjoy the afterlife. Our knowledge of many past civilizations comes directly from their concern with death. This golden bull's head from around 2500 BC adorned a lyre (a stringed musical instrument). It was found in a royal grave site in the Sumerian city of Ur.

Not surprisingly, history gives a special place to civilizations that have left behind a wealth of buildings and artifacts for us to examine and admire. But this can give a distorted picture. Many peoples of the past made buildings and objects out of materials that have not survived. Other cultures became "civilized" without building great cities at all. We have included those that were of lasting significance in this book.

"I was struck dumb with amazement."

This is how the British archaeologist Howard Carter (1873-1939) described the moment when he looked into the tomb of Tutankhamen for the first time in 1922. The tomb was packed full of all kinds of objects—carved furniture, chariots, thrones, sculptures, wall paintings, baskets, and ointment jars. They had remained in the tomb of this young Egyptian king, virtually untouched, since his death in about 1323 BC.

There were greater surprises to come, as Carter and his team of Egyptian workers carefully explored each chamber of the tomb in turn. The tomb included three other rooms as well as the one in which the body lay. The body itself bore a solid gold mask. It was enclosed in a gold coffin, which was itself inside two other gold-covered wooden coffins and a stone sarcophagus (coffin). The tomb was one of the greatest archaeological finds of all time.

The ancient Egyptians did everything possible to protect the tombs from robbers. After about 1550 BC they hid them in the Valley of the Kings, near Thebes. But this did not prevent the tombs from being robbed. All 33 found by Carter's time had been ransacked.

Left Charlemagne's bejeweled tomb was completed in 1215, after 50 years of work. Such great treasures can provide useful clues about the way a civilization spent its wealth, and also tells us what things were considered most important.

Above In Egypt some farmers still use shadufs to raise water from the Nile to irrigate their fields. This technique was used by the ancient Egyptians 5,000 years ago, and is pictured in wall-paintings in tombs.

Below In all cultures, many artifacts are made of materials that will not last, unless they are very carefully preserved like this North American Indian mask. Such items are intended to be used, and when they are worn out or no longer needed they are discarded. Archaeologists often have to piece together history from what survives. But what survives may not be representative of a culture as a whole. Think of all the things that we use and then discard. How will future archaeologists assess our world?

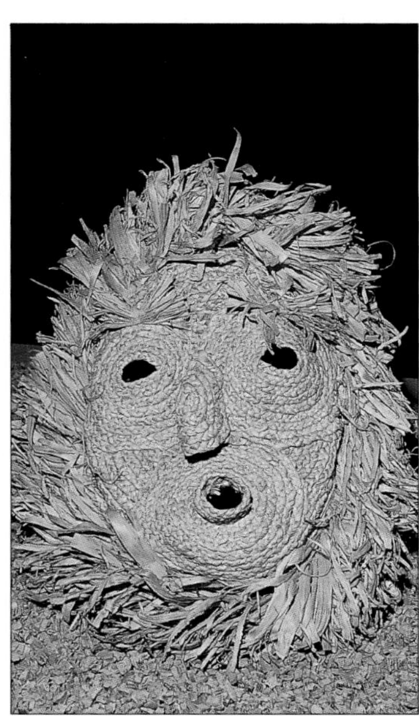

Vanishing history

It is wrong to conclude that a society which leaves virtually nothing behind is necessarily less sophisticated than one that does. Its people still live within a complex and disciplined social structure, and value intelligence and learning. They have their own forms of artistic expression in craftsmanship, music, and dance, but there may be nothing to show for it a thousand years later.

This is a reconstruction of an Irish crannog—a type of lake-island refuge that was inhabited over a period of 2,500 years. Once abandoned a crannog left little trace of busy village life because the buildings and artifacts were made of materials that decayed.

SECTION 2: BEFORE CIVILIZATIONS

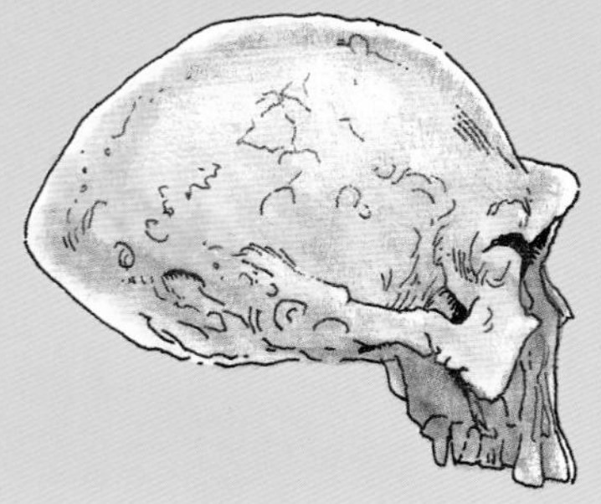

The history of human beings is at least 500 times longer than the history of civilizations. In fact, civilization is comparatively recent. Even modern man, *Homo sapiens sapiens*, took 35,000 years to develop settled agriculture, the foundation stone of civilization.

THE EVOLUTION OF HOMO SAPIENS

The earliest forms of human beings probably lived in Africa some 4 to 6 million years ago. After passing through various stages of evolution, our modern form of human being, *Homo sapiens sapiens,* developed about 40,000 years ago from *Homo erectus* (see box).

Homo sapiens sapiens had a larger brain, but in the beginning followed the same pattern of life. They hunted animals, gathered roots and berries, and often lived in caves for shelter and protection. They also used fire. Their talent for tool-making set human beings apart from other animals. At first, tools and weapons were made with wood and stone.

It was not until about 9000 BC that some of these hunter-gatherers started to farm to provide food. Farming meant that people could settle close to their fields. Small farming communities became villages, and successful villages, with perhaps a market and a temple, became towns.

As far as we know, the earliest towns were in the Near East. Jericho was founded in about 7,000 BC, and Çatal Hüyük in about 6700 BC. But these were not yet major cities, and this was still the Stone Age. Another 3,000 years passed before the first true civilizations emerged—the history of civilization covers only the last 6,000 years of human existence.

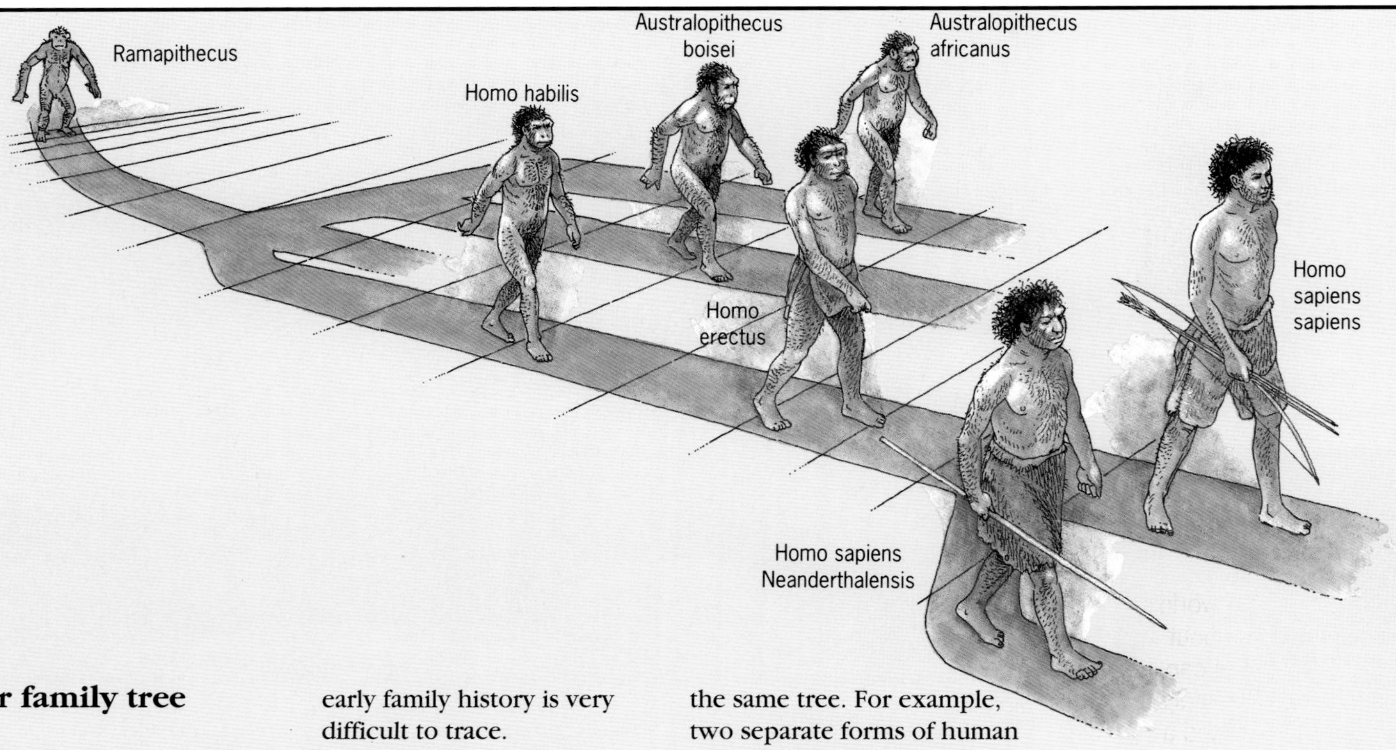

Our family tree

In 1859 a British naturalist, Charles Darwin, published a book about his theory of evolution. This theory showed how human beings could have developed from apelike ancestors that lived millions of years ago. But our early family history is very difficult to trace.

Paleontologists (people who study the history of early human forms) depend on patchy evidence provided by fossils. While some early forms of human beings are our direct ancestors, others are on separate branches of the same tree. For example, two separate forms of human being developed from *Homo erectus*: *Homo sapiens sapiens* (our own form) and *Homo sapiens Neanderthalensis* (Neanderthals), who disappeared about 30,000 years ago.

Early art

Some of the oldest surviving pieces of art are cave paintings. This picture of a bison, from a cave in southern France, is about 30,000 years old. The paintings often showed animals, human beings, patterns, mythical creatures, and supernatural beings. The paints were based on various colored earths. The bison, wounded by arrows, may simply have told the story of a memorable hunt; or perhaps it was a sacred drawing intended to bring success to the hunt. Other drawings may have been intended to ensure the fertility of herds.

Right Early forms of human beings probably spread out from Africa into southern Asia about a million years ago. They moved into northern Europe and the Americas only toward the end of the last Ice Age 70,000-10,000 years ago.

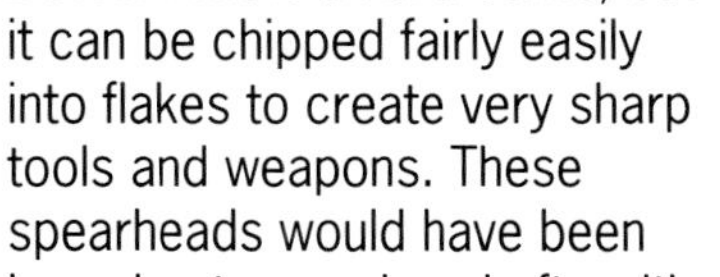

Above *The Venus of Willendorf*, one of the world's oldest sculptures, is about 25,000 years old. It is carved out of limestone. The sculpture was found in Austria, and a number of similar female figures have been found at other places in western Europe. These Venus figures, named after the much later Roman goddess, are thought to be fertility symbols, representing motherhood and childbirth.

Below Flint is a hard stone, but it can be chipped fairly easily into flakes to create very sharp tools and weapons. These spearheads would have been bound onto wooden shafts with leather or twine.

Stone Age town

Çatal Hüyük, in southern central Turkey, is the site of one of the world's earliest towns. In about 6700 BC it grew up as a major agricultural market and trading center. The closely-packed houses were built of mud-brick. People entered them through holes in the roof. Çatal Hüyük also had many religious shrines with elaborate carved and painted interiors.

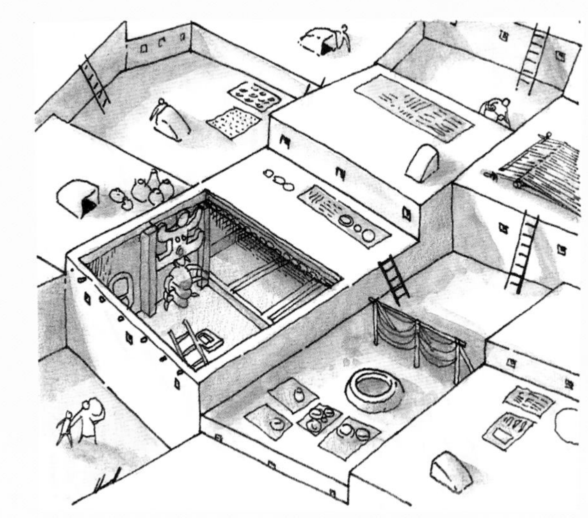

SECTION 3: THE FIRST CIVILIZATIONS

Mesopotamia, ancient Egypt, the Indus Valley, and Ancient China were the world's earliest civilizations. These, and other important civilizations, grew up on the banks of major rivers. The fertile land beside the rivers made it possible for the people to farm successfully.

The royal tombs at Ur

By about 3500 BC the Sumerian city of Ur, on the Euphrates River, was a major trading city. It was also a religious center, with a ziggurat and shrine devoted to Nanna, god of the moon.

The ruins were excavated in the 1920s by the British archaeologist Sir Leonard Woolley. In the Royal Cemetery he discovered tombs of kings and queens filled with all kinds of treasures, including jewelry, ornaments, and musical instruments. The famous statue of the "ram in a thicket" (above) is made of gold, shell, and lapis lazuli. It dates from about 2500 BC.

Woolley made a chilling discovery when he found the bodies of dozens of soldiers and servants who had committed sucide in order to join their kings and queens. Cups that had contained poison still lay beside their skeletons.

THE SUMERIANS AND AKKADIANS

By 5000 BC farming communities were flourishing in Mesopotamia on the fertile land along the banks of the Tigris and Euphrates rivers. Mesopotamia means "land between rivers." By about 3000 BC some of the towns in the south—such as Erech, Kish, Lagash, and Ur—had developed into powerful city-states. These were known collectively as Sumer, but each of the cities was independent. The cities, which were ruled by kings and queens and governments, had walls to keep out enemies. Temples to the gods and palaces were built on top of great stepped pyramids called ziggurats. The Sumerians made tools, weapons, and ornaments from copper, bronze, and gold. They were perhaps the first people to make wheeled vehicles.

In about 2370 BC King Sargon I of Akkad, a city of northern Mesopotamia, conquered Sumer and created an empire that lasted for about 200 years. Later both Sumer and Akkad became part of the Babylonian Empire of Hammurabi (see pages 20-21).

Left Many votive statues have been found at temple sites. Votive statues hold or present something, and were placed in the temple by worshippers as a way of asking for protection from the gods. Each Sumerian city had a patron god. This limestone votive statue of a Sumerian lady was probably carved in about 2500 BC.

Five thousand years of tradition

The key to the civilizations that developed in Mesopotamia was the rivers. They flooded in spring and spread rich silt over the land. The water was used to irrigate the fields through systems of dams and canals. There was no stone in Sumer suitable for building, so mud bricks had to be used. The Sumerians originally built houses of reeds from the rivers. This tradition survives in the marshes between the Tigris and the Euphrates in southern Iraq. Here the Marsh Arabs still build houses with reeds in the same style as their Sumerian ancestors.

Above This beautifully made game board, complete with 14 counters, was found in one of the graves of the Royal Cemetery of Ur. Just how the game was played is not clear.

Below The courses of the Tigris and the Euphrates were different in ancient times. Nippur, Lagash, and Ur were all on the Euphrates, which has since moved away from them. Also, the Gulf stretched inland almost as far as Ur.

From pictures to writing

The Sumerians developed the first system of writing about 3300 BC. Their writing is called cuneiform, meaning "wedge-shaped." They used a wedge-shaped tool, which they pressed into slabs of damp clay. Early texts were usually records of fields and crops. Later, cuneiform was used to write letters and stories.

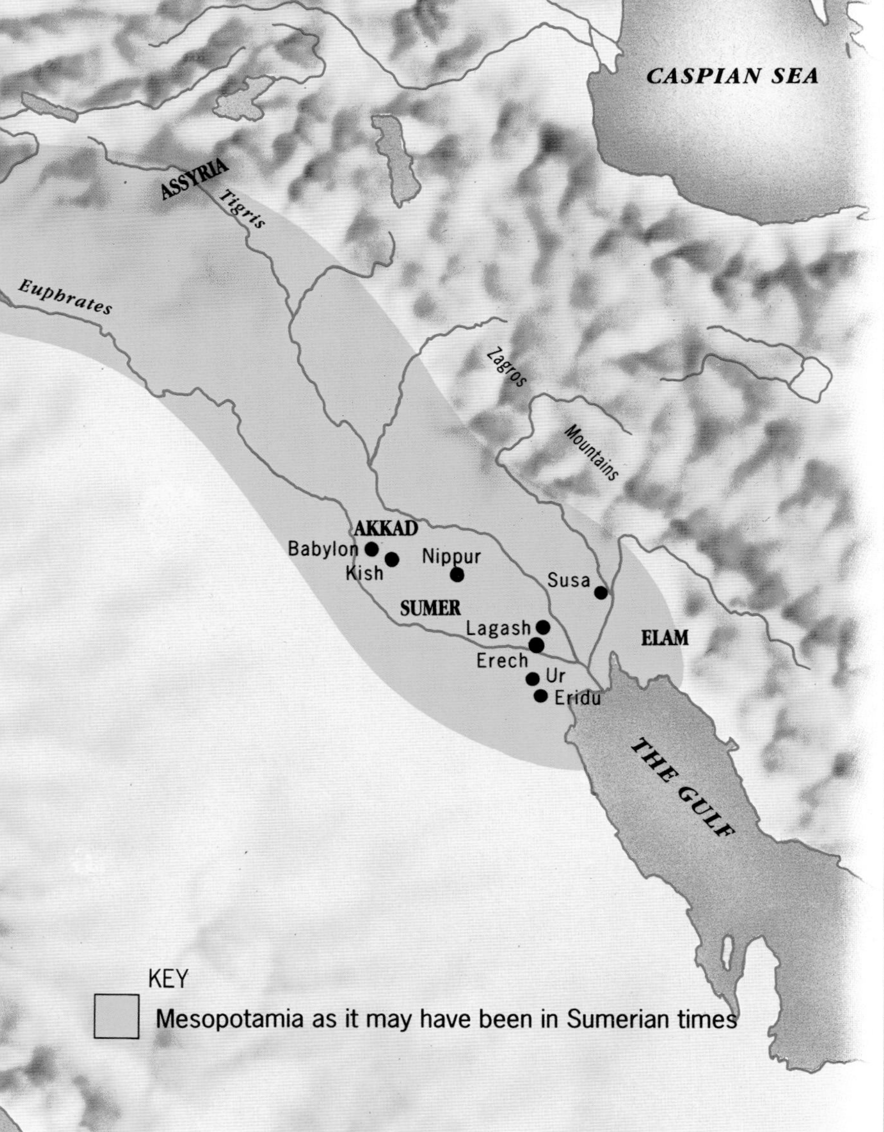

ANCIENT EGYPT

Left This gold mask was found on the mummy of Tutankhamen. It is one of hundreds of magnificent treasures that was found when his tomb was discovered in 1922.

Around 3100 BC King Menes united the lands of Upper and Lower Egypt. The civilization of ancient Egypt grew up on the banks of the Nile River. It lasted about 3,000 years, divided into three main periods.

In the Old Kingdom (about 2686-2181 BC) the capital city was Memphis in northern Egypt. The pyramids were built during this time. Their construction, which involved thousands of laborers, showed just how well organized Egyptian society was. Following a period of turmoil, the Middle Kingdom (2050-1800 BC) emerged, reunited by a prince from Thebes in southern Egypt.

Egypt was occupied by the Hyksos people from 1640-1552 BC. After they were driven out, Egyptian civilization reached a high point of power and wealth during the New Kingdom. From 1085 BC, however, Egypt was invaded by a series of foreign powers, including Assyria (see pages 22-23) and Persia (see pages 30-31). In 332 BC, Alexander the Great (see pages 42-43) conquered Egypt, starting a period of Greek-influenced rule under a series of kings named Ptolemy.

Egyptians believed that life after death was very similar to life on Earth. They buried all kinds of goods with their dead rulers and nobles—not only jewelry and treasures, but weapons, games, even food and seeds. They also wrote their records in hieroglyphics and painted pictures of their lives on the walls of tombs. These sources give us a detailed picture of the way the Egyptians lived.

The world's greatest tombs

The pyramids are the tombs of the Egyptian kings. Their shape developed over several centuries. The step pyramid at Saqqara, built for King Djoser in about 2630 BC, is one of the earliest. The most famous pyramids are at Giza, just outside modern Cairo. The largest is the tomb of King Khufu (or Cheops), which was built around 2500 BC.

Pyramids were supposed to provide a safe place to preserve a king's body, but they proved to be much too easy to rob. In later years royal tombs were hidden away in the Valley of the Kings near Thebes.

Above Great temples and tombs in ancient Egypt were decorated with hundreds of sculptures, many of them portraits of the kings. This statue of Akhenaton, who reigned 1367-1350 BC, shows the symbols of kingship. He is wearing a false beard and holds a crook and flail. He was a mystical man, who tried to bring about a religious revolution. But the empire fell into chaos during his reign. Akhenaton is thought to be the father of Tutankhamen.

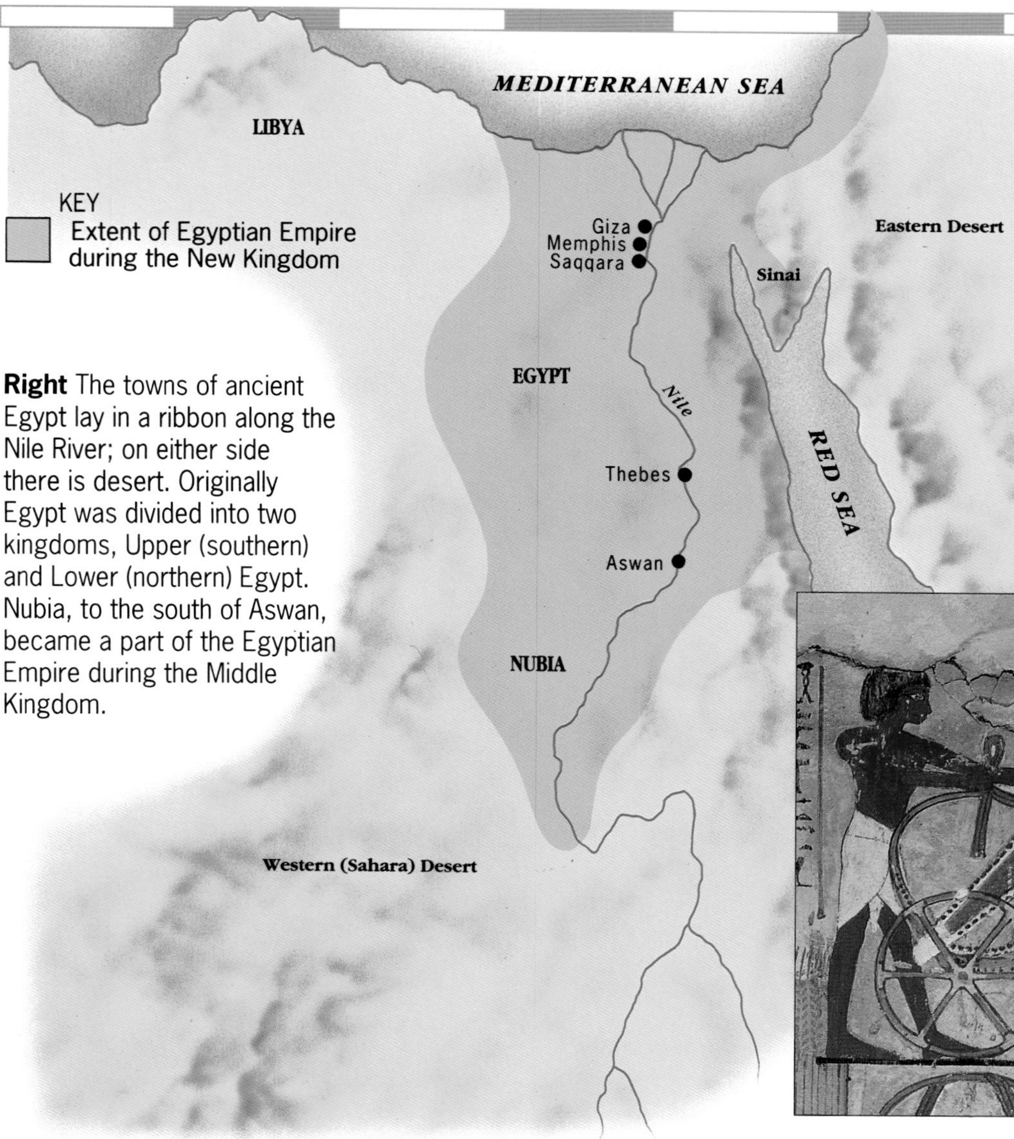

MEDITERRANEAN SEA
LIBYA
KEY
Extent of Egyptian Empire during the New Kingdom
Giza
Memphis
Saqqara
Eastern Desert
Sinai
EGYPT
Nile
RED SEA
Thebes
Aswan
NUBIA
Western (Sahara) Desert

Right The towns of ancient Egypt lay in a ribbon along the Nile River; on either side there is desert. Originally Egypt was divided into two kingdoms, Upper (southern) and Lower (northern) Egypt. Nubia, to the south of Aswan, became a part of the Egyptian Empire during the Middle Kingdom.

Below This picture, painted about 1400 BC, is on the wall of a tomb near Thebes. The swift, light chariot drawn by two horses was introduced to the Egyptians by the Hyksos people. It proved highly effective in war. The Egyptian Empire reached its greatest extent about 1450 BC, when it included the lands of the eastern Mediterranean conquered by Pharaoh Tuthmosis III, who reigned 1490-1436 BC.

The cult of death

The ancient Egyptians believed that there was a life after death. The dead body was embalmed to protect it from decay by using a mineral called natron. It was then wrapped in strips of linen cloth. The preserved mummy had to go through sacred rituals before being placed in a coffin and hidden inside a tomb. Anubis, the jackal-headed god, was believed to oversee these rituals in his role as guide to human souls. This painting on papyrus (a kind of paper made of papyrus reeds), dating from 1300 BC, shows the ceremony called the "opening of the mouth," meant to allow the dead person to breathe, eat, and speak in the afterlife.

Sacred writing

Ancient Egyptian writing is called hieroglyphics, which means sacred carving, because the symbols had religious significance. Hieroglyphics started as picture writing about 3000 BC. Later, some pictures were used to represent the sounds of words. For instance, an owl represented the sound m. There are over 600 symbols in all. Hieroglyphics were a complete mystery until the French scholar Jean-François Champollion deciphered the Rosetta Stone in the 1820s. This large inscribed slab of stone was found near Rosetta in Egypt.

THE INDUS VALLEY

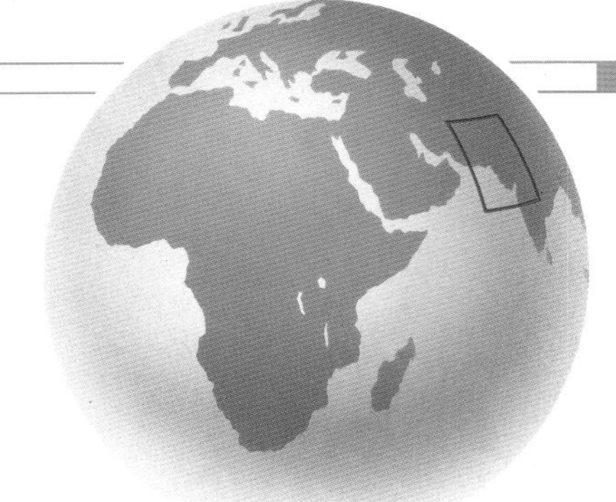

The Indus is one of the great rivers of South Asia, flowing out of the Himalayas into the broad plains of what is now Pakistan. Like the Nile and the rivers of Mesopotamia, it flooded each year, covering the surrounding fields with rich river mud.

By about 5000 BC, people in the Indus Valley lived in settled farming communities. They may have learned the secrets of agriculture through trade with Mesopotamia. In 2500 BC there were about 100 towns and villages and five major cities, the most famous of which are Mohenjo-daro and Harappa.

The Indus Valley civilization was at its height between 2300 and 1700 BC. The people were highly organized. Their cities were planned out in advance, complete with underground sewage systems. Traders used a system of standard weights and measures made of polished stone, which were carefully controlled. Unlike the Sumerians and ancient Egyptians, the Indus Valley people did not build elaborate temples, but they had many small shrines to their gods.

The Indus Valley civilization was virtually unknown until the remains of the cities were discovered in the 1920s. Many aspects of this civilization still remain a mystery, and no one knows why it disappeared around 1700 BC. Perhaps the cities were abandoned when the land became infertile through overuse; or perhaps they were overcome by the Aryans (see pages 62-63), who are known to have conquered this region about 1600 BC.

Trading across the Gulf

The Indus Valley had few raw materials, so these had to be imported from elsewhere. Merchants sailed up the coast and into the Gulf. They used single-masted sailing boats, which were similar to the dhows still used in the Gulf today.

Town planning

The site of the city of Mohenjo-daro shows us just how carefully the town was planned. Two-story brick houses were built around courtyards on streets, laid out on a grid system. Many of them had bathrooms, connected to a sewage system that ran under the streets. There was also a large bath, and it seems likely that bathing played a part in religious ritual. No major grave sites have yet been found, but excavations have revealed jewelry and sculpture (left). The city of Harappa is similar to Mohenjo-daro in many ways. The site was wrecked in the late 19th century when British engineers used the bricks to build a railway.

Below Many clay models have been found in the Indus Valley, such as this bullock cart from Harappa. This suggests that people there knew about the wheel, perhaps through contact with the Sumerian civilization.

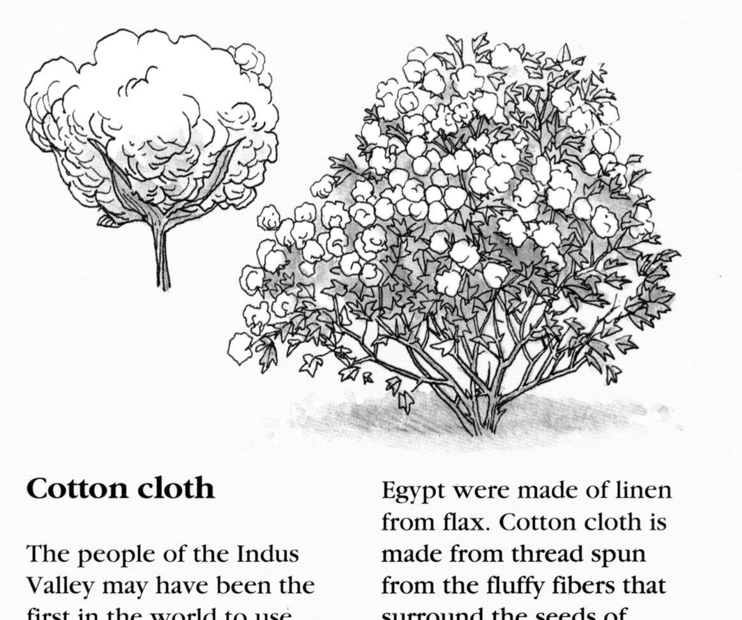

Cotton cloth

The people of the Indus Valley may have been the first in the world to use cotton. Clothes in ancient Egypt were made of linen from flax. Cotton cloth is made from thread spun from the fluffy fibers that surround the seeds of mature cotton plants.

Below These dice, made of cubes of limestone, were found at Mohenjo-daro. Modern dice, made 4,000 years later, use the same patterns of dots to indicate the value of each face. As elsewhere in the ancient world, board games were clearly enjoyed by many people.

Mysterious writing

The people of the Indus Valley used a form of picture writing. So far no one has been able to decipher it. Part of the problem is that the symbols often have several unconnected meanings. A picture of one thing may be used to indicate something very different simply because the words for both things sounded similar. This writing appears on seals, which were used as a signature on clay documents. The seals usually include a picture of an animal, such as the humped bull shown here. The animals may have had religious significance; the bull is an animal associated with the god Shiva.

Below The main cities of Mohenjo-daro and Harappa were 375 miles (600 km) apart. Other cities were closer to each other, such as Chanhu-daro and Kalibangan. Lothal, to the south-west, was a port and a major trading center.

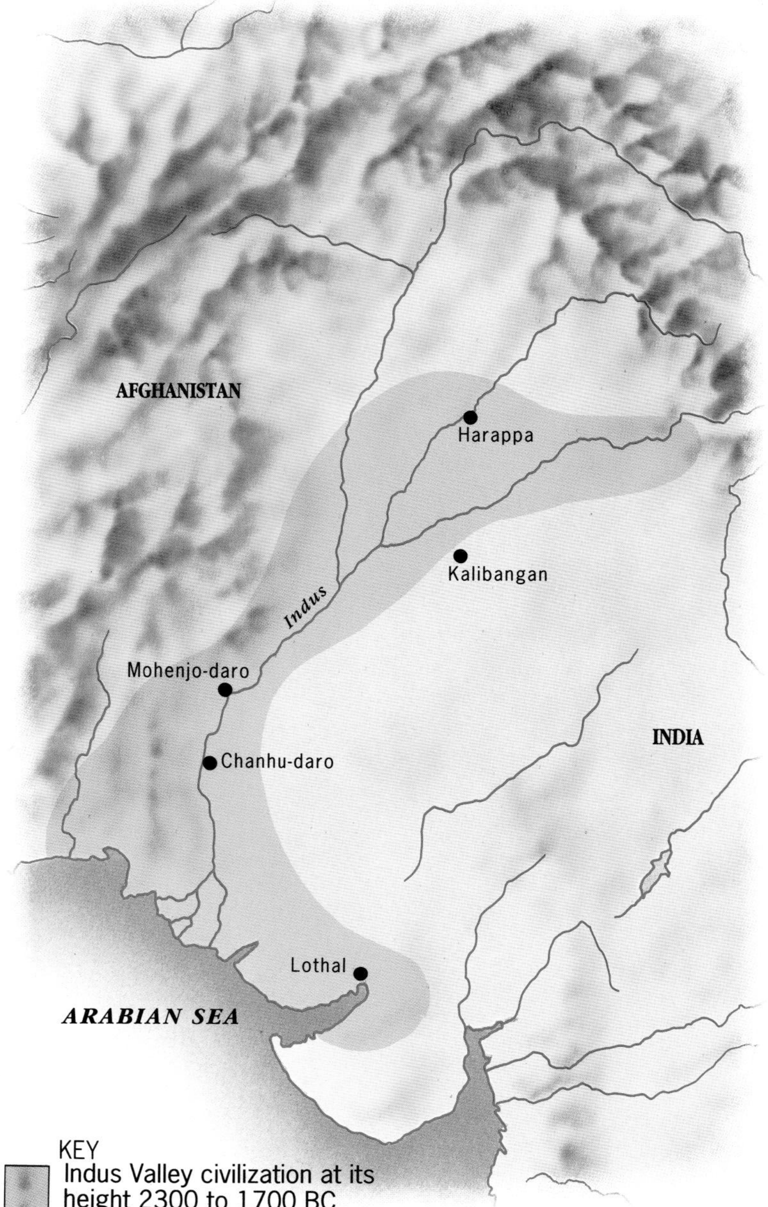

ANCIENT CHINA

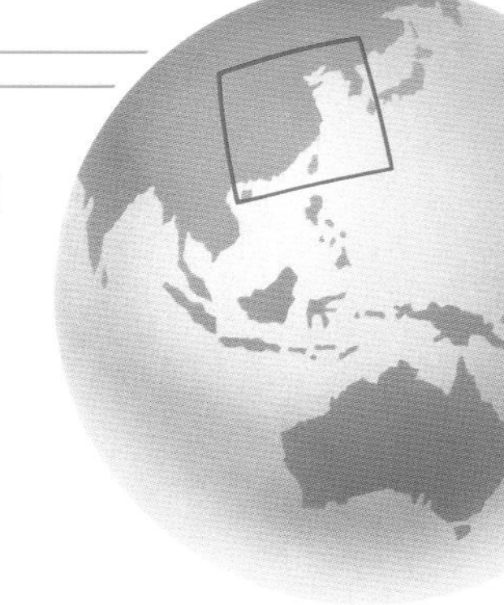

The civilization of ancient China grew up in the valley of the Hwang Ho or Yellow River. The agriculture of the first villages, which were established by 5000 BC, was based on the cultivation of millet. By 2500 BC rice was being grown in the warmer valley of the Yangtze River (Chang Jiang) farther south.

The Hsia Dynasty is thought to be the first dynasty of kings to rule China, from around 2000-1500 BC. During this period, irrigation canals were built to bring water to the fields, and soldiers used chariots and bronze weapons.

The Chinese kings were thought to be the link between the people and the gods. If the king ruled justly and performed the correct rituals, these gods would look after him and his people, and bring stability and harmony to his kingdom. The first cities were built as religious centers for ceremonies and ritual.

By the time of the Shang Dynasty (about 1500-1050 BC) there were a number of cities in China, such as the last Shang capital Yin-Chu (now An-yang). The cities were carefully planned on a grid system—a pattern that all later Chinese capitals followed. The people were organized into grades of social rank, ranging from royalty and nobles to the slaves. The early Chinese excelled in the skill of bronze-casting, and many beautiful bronze vessels have been found in tombs of the Shang Dynasty.

Below This cast-bronze vessel from the Shang period was probably used in ceremonial offerings of food to the ancestor gods. The ancient Chinese cast these vessels in several pieces, using molds pressed from clay models. The patterns represent animal faces.

Although Chinese civilization developed 1,000 years later than the other early civilizations farther west, there are no records of any contact with them. This isolation has shaped China's sense of individuality ever since.

Right The Hwang Ho or Yellow River gets its name from the color of the rich yellow mud that it carries. Each year the river overflowed its banks, and when the floods receded mud was left behind. Crops could be grown and easily watered in this highly fertile soil. The raised land beyond the river, however, often remained dry and infertile. The flooding could also cause widespread damage, earning the Yellow River the nickname "China's Sorrow." The Shang Dynasty had to move its capital five times because of flooding.

Smooth as silk

Silk is an extremely fine cloth made from cocoons spun by the silkworm, the caterpillar of the silk moth. The cocoons are boiled before the thread is harvested—as much as 1,000 yds (9,144 m) per cocoon. According to legend, a loom for weaving silk was invented in China by Empress Hsi Ling Shi in 2640 BC. The secret of how silk was made remained closely guarded, and was known only in China until the 4th century AD. After 120 BC, silk became one of the most valued goods that passed along the trade routes to West Asia and Europe, and these routes became known as the "Silk Roads."

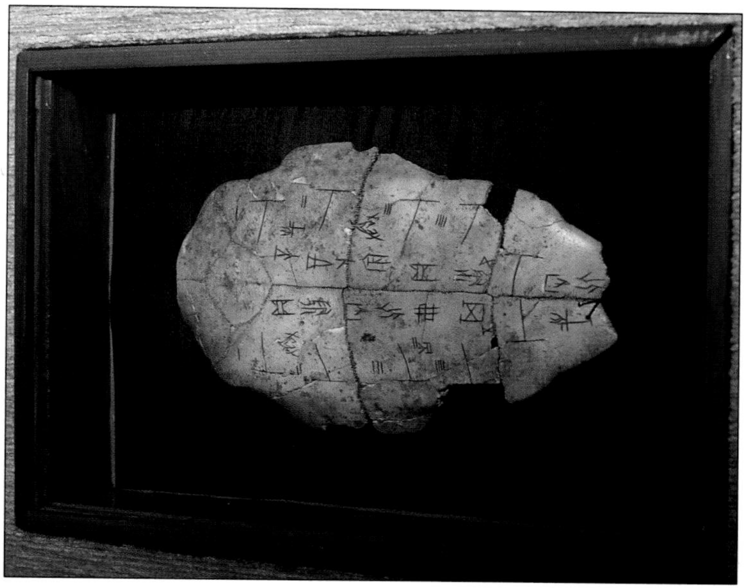

Above The earliest forms of Chinese writing are found on skulls and shoulder blades. These were sacred symbols, used by priests as a way of divining the future. The symbols were a kind of picture writing, but they became increasingly stylized. The characters used in Chinese writing today are derived from these early symbols. Unlike our alphabet, they do not represent sounds, but ideas. In this way all Chinese can read the same writing, even though they may pronounce it differently in their own dialect or language.

Above The Chinese had a gift for pottery, which is evident in this urn dating from the Neolithic period, about 3000 BC. The black coloring is an earth pigment; glazes were introduced during the Shang Dynasty.

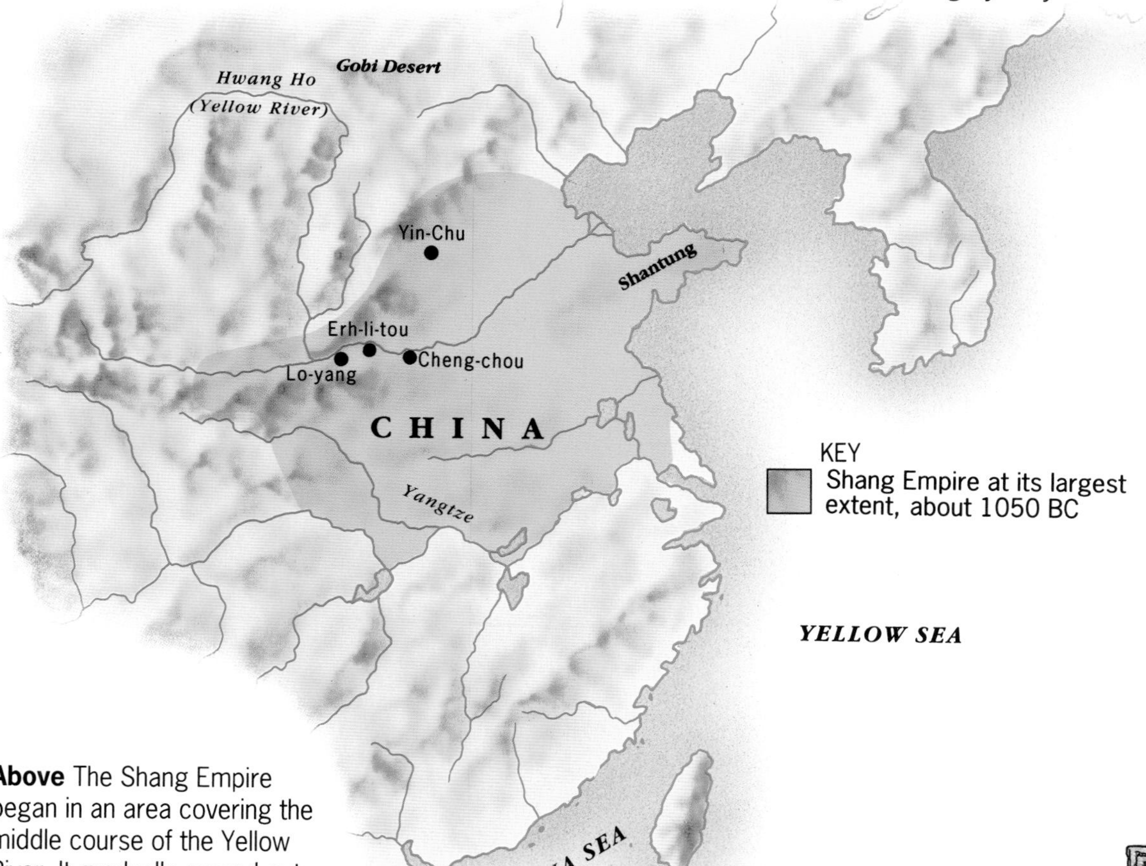

Above The Shang Empire began in an area covering the middle course of the Yellow River. It gradually spread out from there to span all of the lower reaches. It also stretched south to the Yangtze River.

Forever jade

Jade is a semi-precious stone that has been cherished in China since prehistoric times. It is so hard that it cannot be sculpted with a hammer or chisel, but has to be shaped using a rough, abrasive surface. Jade was used for the blades of daggers and axes. Because jade was believed to prevent bodies from decaying, jade objects were often included in burials.

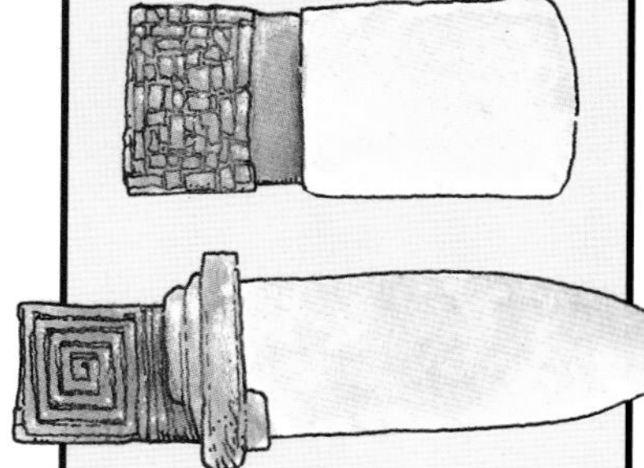

SECTION 4: WEST ASIA

During the time when the great empires in Mesopotamia flourished, the eastern Mediterranean became a vital crossroads. This region was the birthplace of both Judaism and Christianity. In the 7th century AD it was transformed by the arrival of a new religion—Islam.

THE BABYLONIANS

Babylon, on the Euphrates River, became a powerful city after about 1900 BC. Its culture was strongly influenced by the neighboring civilizations of Sumer and Akkad (see pages 12-13), sharing many of their features, such as cuneiform writing and ziggurats.

Under King Hammurabi, who reigned from 1792 to 1750 BC, Babylon acquired an empire. Both Sumer and Akkad came under Babylonian control and Assyria was conquered. Hammurabi is famous for a detailed code of laws drawn up during his reign. He also encouraged the construction of a network of irrigation canals.

After Hammurabi, Babylon suffered a series of conquests by the Hittites (see pages 24-25), Kassites, and Hurrians. Not much is known about the next 1,000 years, but after 721 BC Babylon became part of the Assyrian Empire.

When Assyrian power declined, the Chaldeans of southern Mesopotamia took over and Babylon underwent a major revival under the new Chaldean kings, Nabopolassar (reigned 625-605 BC) and Nebuchadnezzar (reigned 605-562 BC). Nebuchadnezzar extended the Babylonian Empire to the Mediterranean, defeating the Egyptians and the last of the Assyrians at the Battle of Carchemish in 605 BC. He rebuilt Babylon, now a city of 200,000 people, on a magnificent scale.

In 539 BC Babylon fell to a new power in the region—the Persians (see pages 30-31).

Hammurabi the lawmaker

The laws of Hammurabi are recorded on this stone pillar. They deal with taxes, trade, divorce, and debt, as well as crimes such as stealing and murder. The laws showed how society as a whole would apply punishments to wrongdoers, and outlined the rights of any individual to justice. Some of the laws might seem strange to us. For example, if a man owed money to someone, he could lend his wife as a slave. On top of the pillar Hammurabi stands before the Babylonian god of justice, Shamash.

The Hanging Gardens

The Hanging Gardens of Babylon were called one of the Seven Wonders of the Ancient World by the Greek historian and traveler Herodotus (about 484-425 BC). Even in his day, Babylon, under Persian rule, was still a magnificent city. According to legend, the Hanging Gardens were created for a king's young wife who yearned for the green scenery of her mountain homeland. However, there is little evidence of how the gardens actually looked. Possibly they were planted in earth heaped onto the lower terraces of the great ziggurat built during Nebuchadnezzar's time. Certainly the remnants of tree trunks, and holes that could have been used for drainage, were found during excavations earlier in this century.

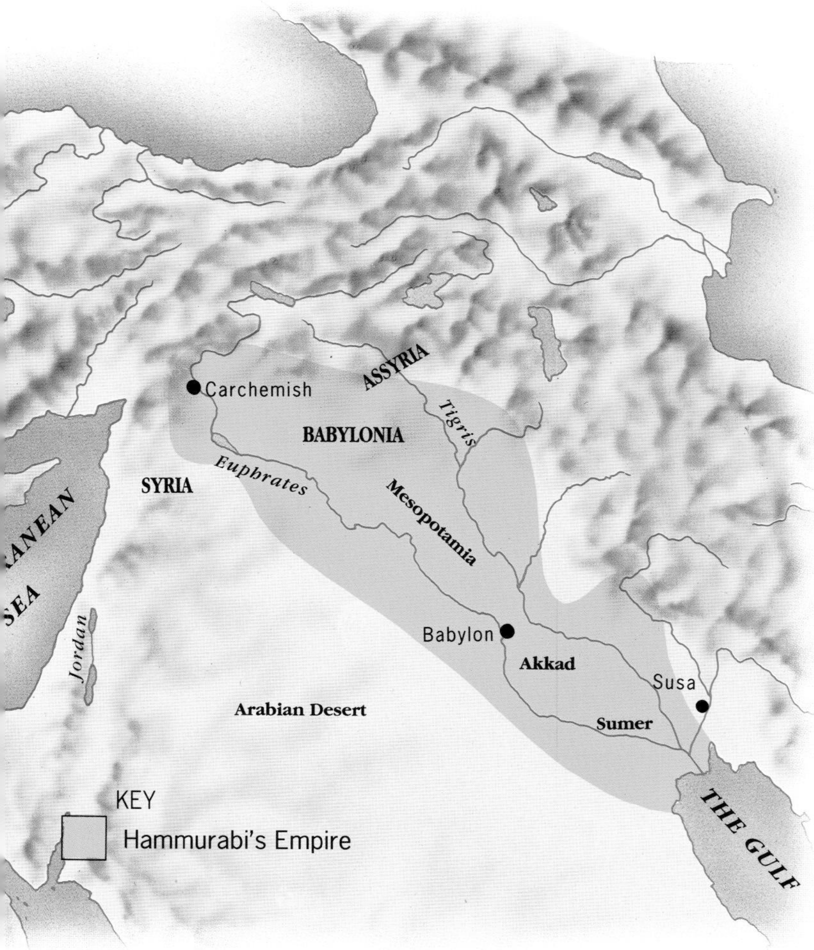

Above Babylon, which lay near the middle of Mesopotamia, was well placed to act as a trading center and the capital of an empire. To the north were the lands of the Assyrians and the Hittites; to the south lay the old cities of Sumer, and access to the sea on the Gulf coast.

Above A magnificent ceremonial walkway, lined with glazed and sculpted tiles, led from the huge Ishtar Gate in Babylon's city walls to the ziggurat built by Nebuchadnezzar. Uncovered in excavations during the 19th century, it has been reconstructed in Berlin.

Making their mark

Like the Sumerians, the Babylonians wrote on clay tablets and rolled seals over their documents as a way of signing them. The seals were cylinders of intricately carved hard stone.

Above This portrait of a king, dating from about 1100 BC, gave authority to one of the many boundary stones that marked out Babylonian territory.

Left The site of Babylon was reconstructed during the 1980s under the orders of President Saddam Hussein of Iraq. The city was once surrounded by a moat filled with water channeled from the Euphrates, but it now sits high and dry because the course of the Euphrates River has changed since ancient times. Although Babylon lay in the middle of the desert, large-scale irrigation made the land around it fertile enough to feed the large population.

THE ASSYRIANS

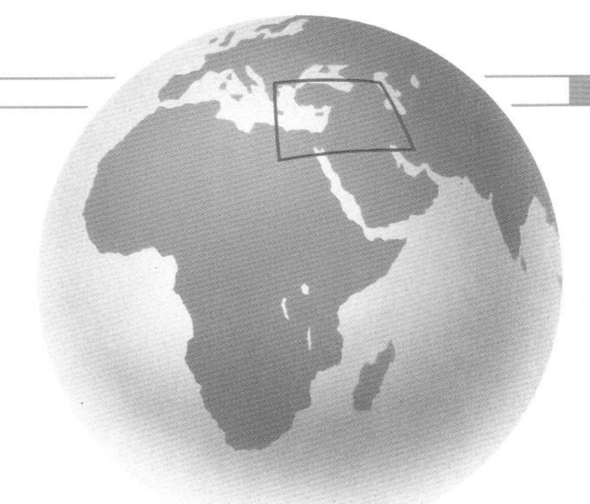

The Assyrians were a warlike nation, named after their original capital on the Tigris River, Ashur (or Assur). Following the centuries of turmoil in Mesopotamia after the reign of Hammurabi in Babylon (see pages 20-21), the Assyrians rose to power and created an empire under a king named Tiglathpileser I, who died about 1074 BC. Assyrian warriors, armed with iron weapons and chariots, quickly won a reputation for their determination and skill.

After a lull, the Assyrian Empire was revived by Ashurnasirpal II (reigned about 883-859 BC), who moved the capital to Calah (Nimrud). Tiglathpileser III (reigned 745-727 BC) then extended the Assyrian territories further by conquering Babylon.

Sennacherib (reigned 705-681 BC) conquered Judea (see pages 28-29), and moved the capital to Nineveh, which became famous for its great wealth and splendor. Nineveh also had a magnificent library filled with cuneiform tablets on history, religion, mathematics, and medicine.

The empire reached its greatest extent under Ashurbanipal (reigned 668-627 BC), and included most of Egypt (see pages 14-15). At its most powerful, the Empire was efficiently organized. But after Ashurbanipal's death, its resources—and the loyalties of its conquered people—were close to exhausted. Nineveh was sacked by the Babylonians, Medes, and Persians (see pages 30-31) in 612 BC, and the territories of Assyria were taken over first by Babylon and then by Persia.

King of beasts

In Assyria lion hunting was reserved for kings alone. By hunting lions, kings could demonstrate their power over the "king of beasts." Here Ashurbanipal is seen shooting with a bow and arrow from his chariot, while the assistants spear a lion attacking them from behind.

This series of relief carvings comes from Ashurbanipal's palace at Nineveh and dates from about 645 BC.

Left Another relief carving from Nineveh shows Ashurbanipal and his queen relaxing with a drink in the garden. Some servants bring them food, while others keep them cool with fans. It looks like a gentle, peaceful scene. But the Assyrians were also noted for their cruelty. In this same sculpture, a little farther to the left, the head of one of Ashurbanipal's enemies can be seen hanging in a tree.

Right Huge winged creatures—half man, half beast—guarded gateways and throne rooms of Assyrian cities. (This one is at Calah.) The heads have horned caps, showing that they are divine beasts—powerful and magnificent monsters who could scare away intruders. They have been sculpted with five legs. Seen from the side, these winged beasts look as though they are walking; seen from the front, they look as though they are standing still.

Below The ivory carvings found at Calah—used mainly as furniture decorations—were probably made by Phoenicians (see pages 26-27), and may have been paid as tribute to their Assyrian rulers.

Left Calah was excavated in the 1840s by the British archaeologist Henry Layard (1817-1894), and the discovery of its palaces, temples, and sculptures caused great excitement throughout the world. Layard later published a book illustrated by very fanciful reconstructions of the city.

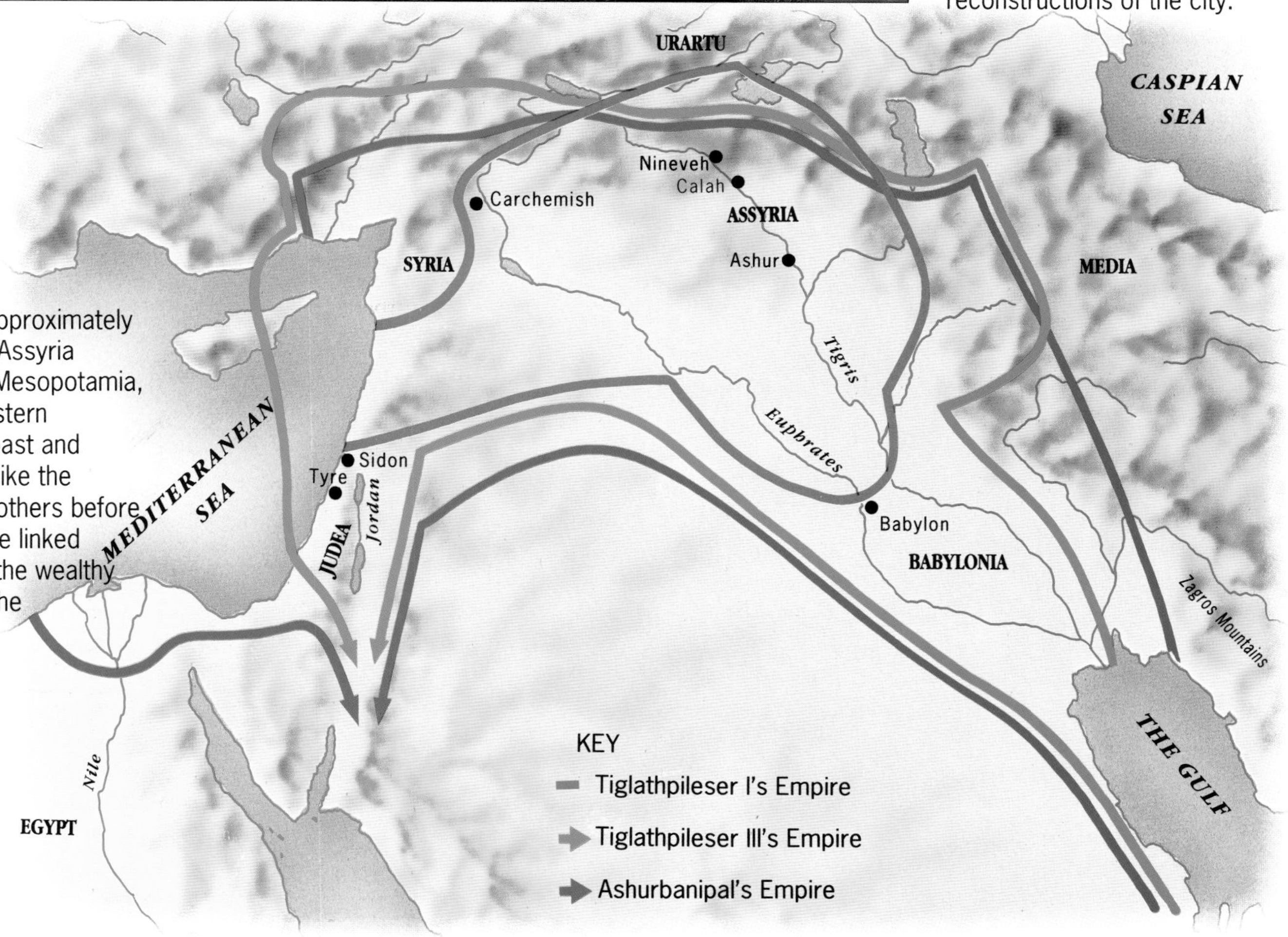

URARTU
CASPIAN SEA
Nineveh
Calah
Carchemish
ASSYRIA
Ashur
SYRIA
MEDIA
Tigris
Euphrates
MEDITERRANEAN SEA
Sidon
Tyre
JUDEA
Jordan
Babylon
BABYLONIA
Zagros Mountains
THE GULF
Nile
EGYPT

KEY
Tiglathpileser I's Empire
Tiglathpileser III's Empire
Ashurbanipal's Empire

Right Between approximately 880 and 626 BC Assyria dominated all of Mesopotamia, as well as the eastern Mediterranean coast and northern Egypt. Like the Babylonians and others before them, their empire linked Mesopotamia to the wealthy lands bordering the Mediterranean.

THE HITTITES

The Hittite people are thought to have come from the Caucasus—the mountainous region between the Black Sea and the Caspian Sea—and settled in what is now eastern Turkey around 2000 BC. By about 1800 BC they had founded a capital at Hattusas (called Boghazkoy today), and soon began to forge an empire for themselves by conquering the lands of the eastern Mediterranean. In 1595 BC King Mursilis I defeated the Kassite rulers of Babylon (see pages 20-21).

However, future generations of Hittites concentrated on the corner of western Asia nearer their homelands, which they dominated from 1500 to 1200 BC. During this time the Egyptian Empire stretched up the eastern Mediterranean coast to the lands of the Mitanni. An uneasy balance of power was sustained until the Hittite King Suppiluliumas (reigned about 1380-1350 BC) conquered the Mitanni people. The Hittite Empire now reached its greatest extent.

Pharaoh Rameses II of Egypt clashed with the Hittites at the Battle of Kadesh in 1285 BC, but later signed a peace treaty with them and married a Hittite princess. However, the so-called Sea-Peoples—raiders from the north who menaced all of the eastern Mediterranean—overran the Hittites in about 1200 BC, and destroyed Hattusas. The Hittites who survived, notably around the city of Carchemish on the Euphrates River, are known as Neo-Hittites. They were conquered by the Assyrians (see pages 22-23) in 717 BC.

Below The Yazilikaya, the national shrine, was set a short distance above Hattusas. It features some of the finest Hittite relief carving, including this frieze of the "twelve gods," wearing conical hats and brandishing curved swords.

A mighty city

Hattusas was first founded around 3000 BC on a hillside overlooking fertile lands, supplied by natural springs, and well placed to be a trading center. It was the Hittite capital and reached its greatest magnificence during the reign of King Tudhaliya about 1250 BC. Hattusas was defended by huge walls stretching 4 miles (6.4 km), and by almost 200 towers.

The lower wall was pierced by three gates, including the massive "Lion Gate," named after the sculptures that guard it. The city contained a number of temples as well as a royal citadel, in which thousands of clay records were discovered. These include the Treaty of Kadesh signed with the Egyptians in 1259 BC.

Right The Hittite Empire covered most of modern Turkey and Syria. Under Suppiluliumas's successor, Mursilis II, it may even have stretched westward as far as the Aegean Sea.

Below The Hittites had their own form of picture writing, or hieroglyphics, which was carved in relief on stone. They also adapted the cuneiform writing of Mesopotamia to their own language.

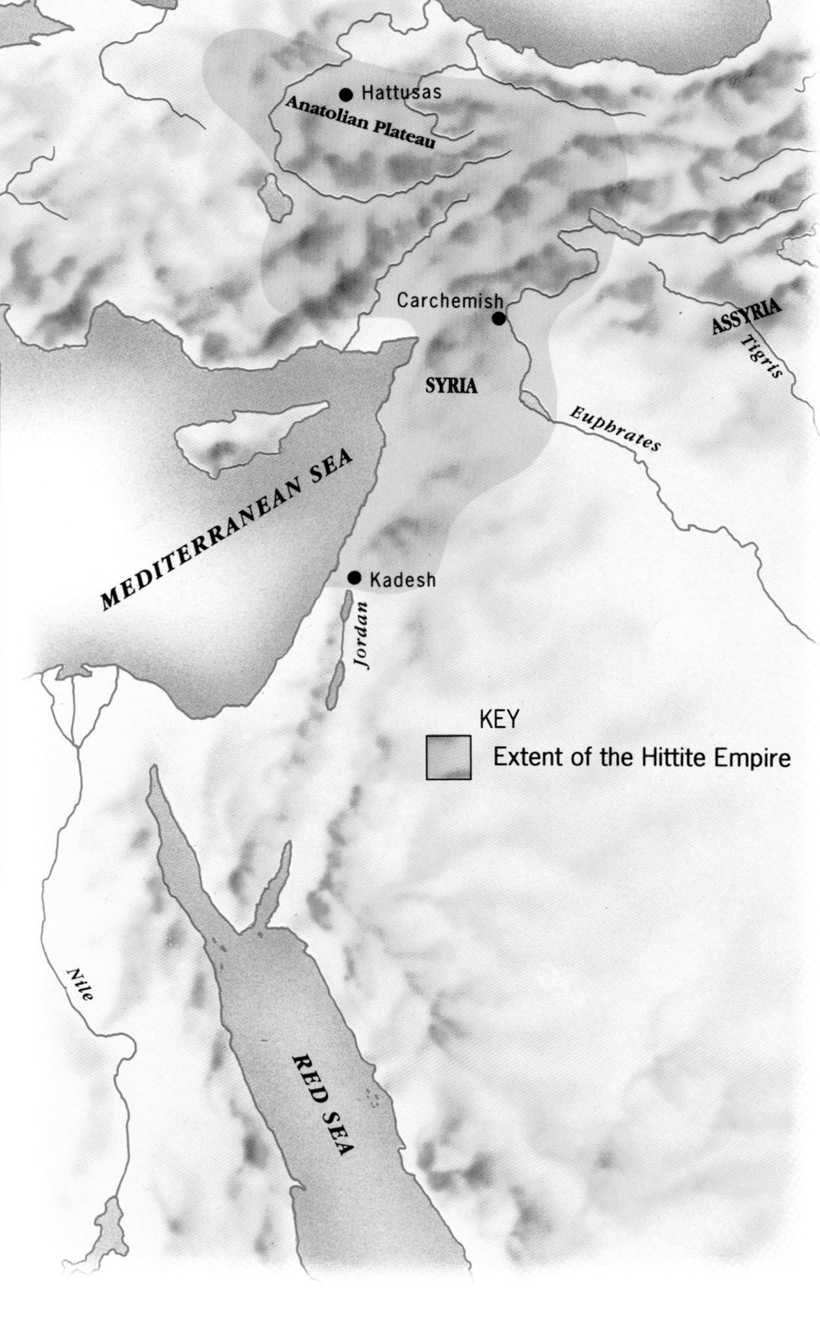

Left The Neo-Hittites carried on many of the traditions of the earlier Hittite culture from their centers in Syria. This relief sculpture reflects the fact that their lands, divided into small kingdoms, were constantly under threat and had to be defended—on horseback and with horse-drawn chariots.

Right This stone sculpture from northeastern Syria clearly shows the influence of West Asian style on Neo-Hittite art. The neatly curled hair and beard echo Mesopotamian portraits, while the wide-open eyes were often a feature of Phoenician sculpture.

THE PHOENICIANS

The Phoenicians were the greatest traders of the ancient world, and they dominated Mediterranean trade from about 1200 to 300 BC. Originally they were Canaanites who lived along the fertile coasts of the eastern Mediterranean. Growing rich from trade, several of their cities became powerful city-states, notably Tyre and Sidon.

The Phoenicians set up trading posts in various parts of the Mediterranean. The most famous was Carthage in north Africa, which was a major Mediterranean power by the 7th century BC. There were other important settlements at Utica near Carthage, Cadiz in southern Spain, and on the islands of Cyprus, Rhodes, and Ibiza. There was no such thing as a Phoenician Empire, however. The city-states in Phoenicia itself, and the settlements abroad, were all more or less independent.

Phoenicia was at the crossroads of the ancient empires and the Phoenicians were frequently ruled by conquerors, including the Egyptians (see pages 14-15), the Assyrians (see pages 22-23), and the Persians (see pages 30-31). The Phoenicians were such successful merchants that occupying powers usually demanded tribute from them but otherwise let them go about their business.

After defeat by Alexander the Great in 330 BC, however, Phoenicia became part of the Hellenistic world (see pages 42-43), and lost its distinctive language and culture. Carthage was destroyed by the Romans in 146 BC.

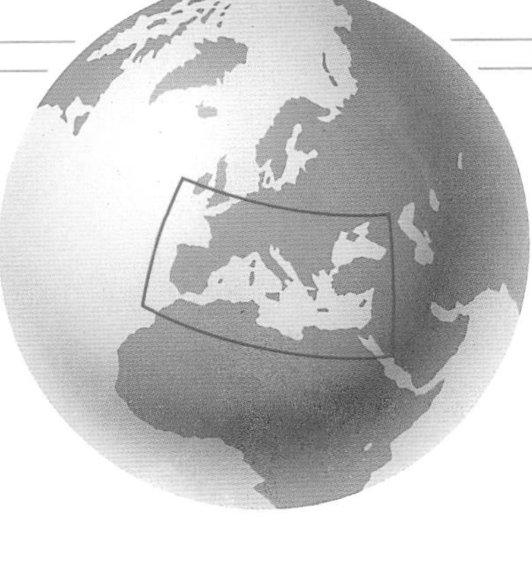

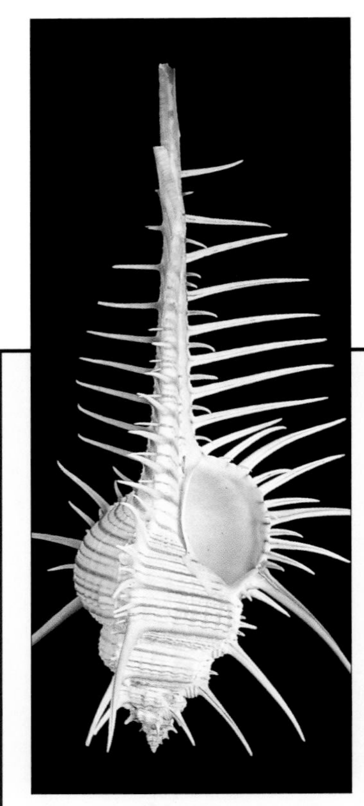

The color purple

The name "Phoenician" may come from the Greek word *phoinikes*, meaning "purple men." The Phoenicians discovered how to make a purple dye from a shellfish called murex. This dye was expensive, and admired in the ancient world. In Rome the emperor wore a purple toga.

Above For centuries the Phoenicians were the best shipbuilders and seafarers of the Mediterranean. Their sturdy trading vessels transported grain, spices, cloth, pottery, glass, jewelry, metals, slaves, and carved ivory. Cedar wood, which came from the Lebanon mountains, was the most valuable of Phoenicia's own exports.

From papyrus to books

Phoenician trading connections spanned the Mediterranean. Merchants from Byblos (left) bought papyrus, an early kind of paper, from Egypt and then sold it to Greek traders. In fact, Byblos became so well known for this trade that the Greeks called papyrus *biblos*, and a book *biblion*.

Right The Phoenicians were gifted craftsmen, known for their ivory carvings. The Assyrian kings used Phoenician ivories to decorate the furniture in the sumptuous palace at Calah in the 8th century BC. This one, of a lion mauling a man, was set with semi-precious stones—blue lapis lazuli and red carnelians.

Left Glass was another luxury item produced by the Phoenicians. They learned how to make glass from the Egyptians. But whereas Egyptian glass was cloudy, the Phoenicians were able to make clear glass, using the sand from their shores, which is rich in quartz. As a result, their beautiful glassware was much in demand.

How the alphabet began

Most early civilizations developed a form of writing based on pictures. Everything needed a separate picture. A system based on sounds is much more efficient. As there are only about 30 different sounds in speech, any word can be written down using a system of 30 letters or less. The Phoenicians developed a system of 22 letters. The first letter was called aleph, meaning "ox," and the second was called beth, "house." The Greeks adapted the Phoenician alphabet, calling their first letter alpha and the second beta. Our own alphabet is based on Roman letters adapted from the Greek.

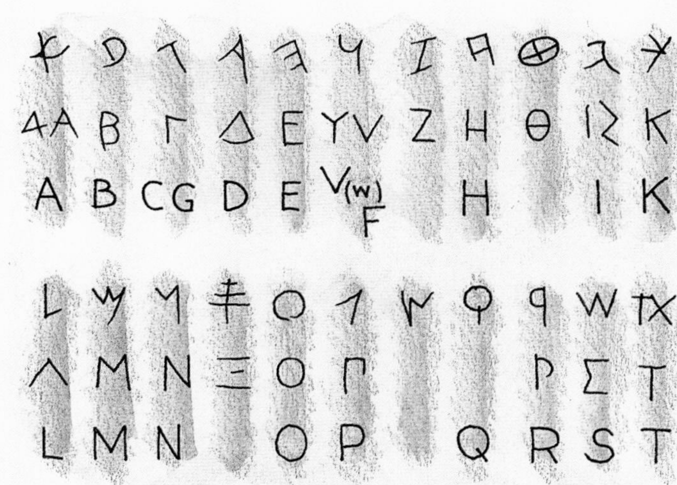

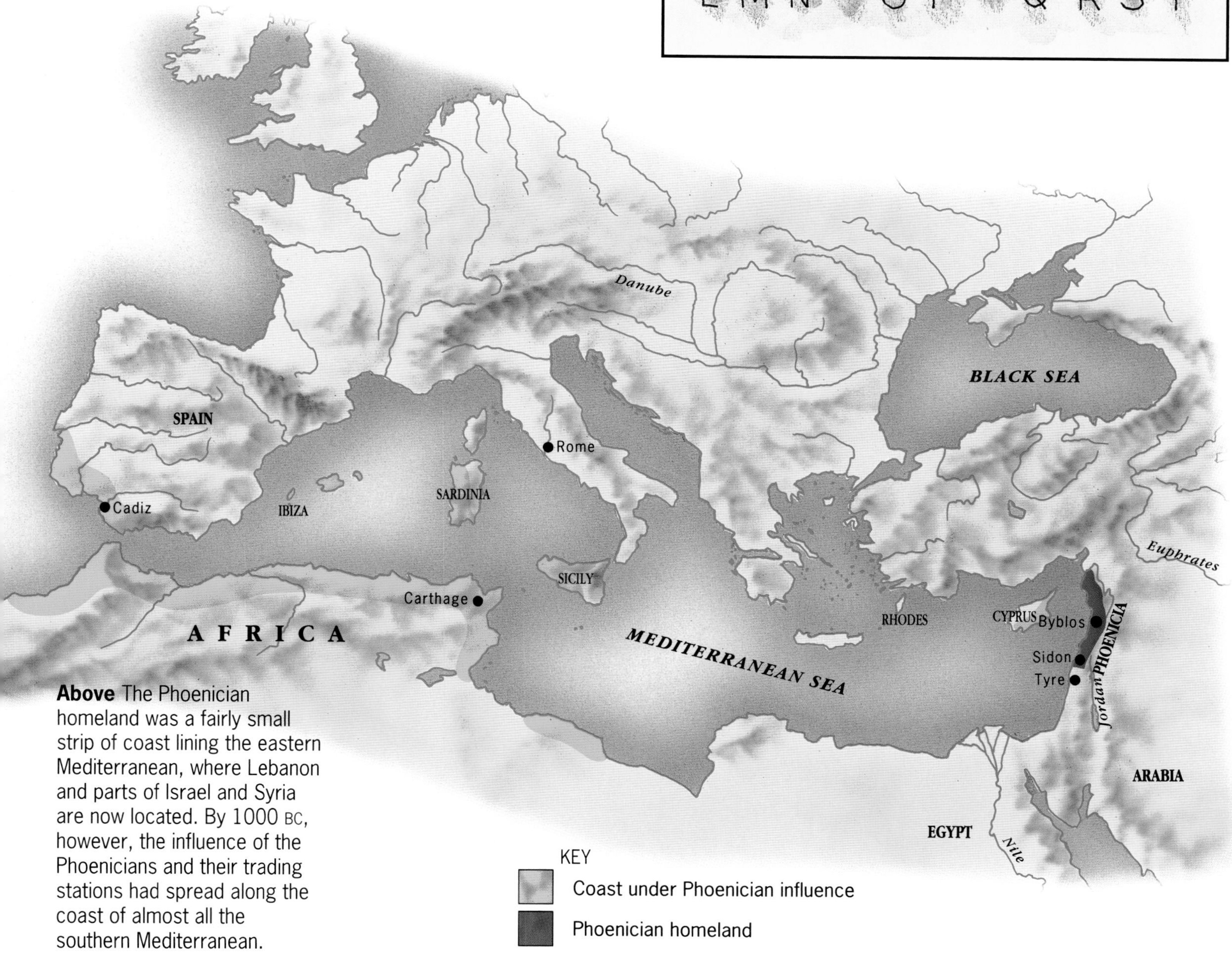

SPAIN
Cadiz
IBIZA
SARDINIA
Rome
Danube
SICILY
Carthage
AFRICA
MEDITERRANEAN SEA
BLACK SEA
RHODES
CYPRUS
Byblos
Sidon
Tyre
PHOENICIA
Jordan
Euphrates
ARABIA
EGYPT
Nile

KEY
Coast under Phoenician influence
Phoenician homeland

Above The Phoenician homeland was a fairly small strip of coast lining the eastern Mediterranean, where Lebanon and parts of Israel and Syria are now located. By 1000 BC, however, the influence of the Phoenicians and their trading stations had spread along the coast of almost all the southern Mediterranean.

THE HEBREWS

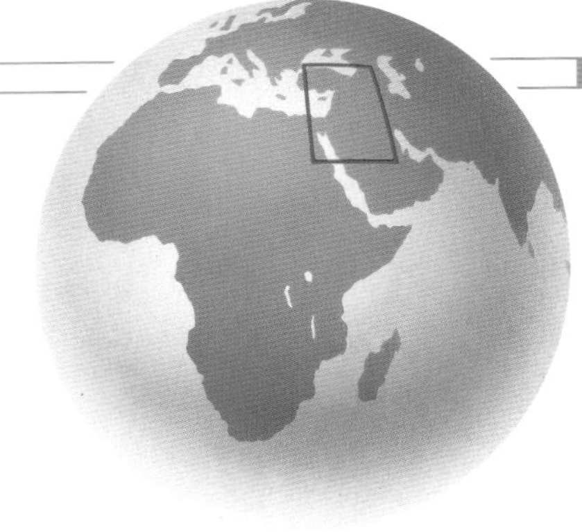

The Hebrews traced their ancestry back to Abraham. He is believed to have come from Mesopotamia (see pages 12-13) to Canaan, on the Mediterranean coast, about 1900 BC. Some of the Hebrew tribes went to live in Egypt (see pages 14-15), but when their lives became intolerable under a pharaoh thought to be Rameses II (about 1304-1237 BC), they were led back to Canaan by Moses. Moses insisted on the worship of one god only, while all the other peoples of the region worshipped many. The Hebrews gradually adopted the complex set of written laws found in the *Torah,* the first five books of the Bible.

King David (reigned about 1012-972 BC) expanded their territory, but after the death of his son Solomon (reigned about 972-922 BC) the kingdom split into two parts—Israel and Judea (named after the tribe of Judah, the great-grandson of Abraham, and the origin of the word Jew).

Israel was conquered by the Assyrians (see pages 22-23) in 722 BC and its people scattered, then by the Babylonians (see pages 20-21), who sacked Jerusalem in 587 BC. Many of the Jews were taken to Babylon in what is called the Babylonian Captivity. This lasted until 538 BC when the Babylonians were conquered by the Persians.

After Alexander the Great took over Judea in 334 BC, the Judeans lived in peace. The unpopular rule of Antiochus Epiphanes of Syria resulted in a successful rebellion in 166 BC, led by Judas Maccabeus. His family then ruled an independent Judea for a century, until it was conquered by the Romans (see pages 46-47) in 63 BC.

Below This Hebrew inscription comes from a tomb of the early 7th century BC. It could well have been the overly elaborate tomb for which a royal steward, Shebna, was rebuked in the Bible (Book of Isaiah, 22:15,16).

The Western Wall

This wall in Jerusalem is one of the most sacred places of Judaism. It is said to be the last remnant of the Temple of Herod, which was destroyed by the Romans in AD 70. Jews come here to offer prayers, and to grieve over the destruction of the temple (hence its more familiar name, the "Wailing Wall").

There had been three great temples on or near this site. The first was built by King Solomon, but destroyed by the Babylonians in 587 BC. Another was built at the end of the Babylonian Captivity. The third was the huge temple, covering 19 acres (7.7 hectares), built by King Herod the Great about 20 BC.

The Dead Sea Scrolls

The Old Testament of the Bible is essentially a book about the laws, religion, and history of the Hebrews. It was written in the Hebrew language between 1200 and 150 BC. In 1947 the oldest known copies of text from it, dating from between 100 BC and 100 AD, were found in a cave near the Dead Sea.

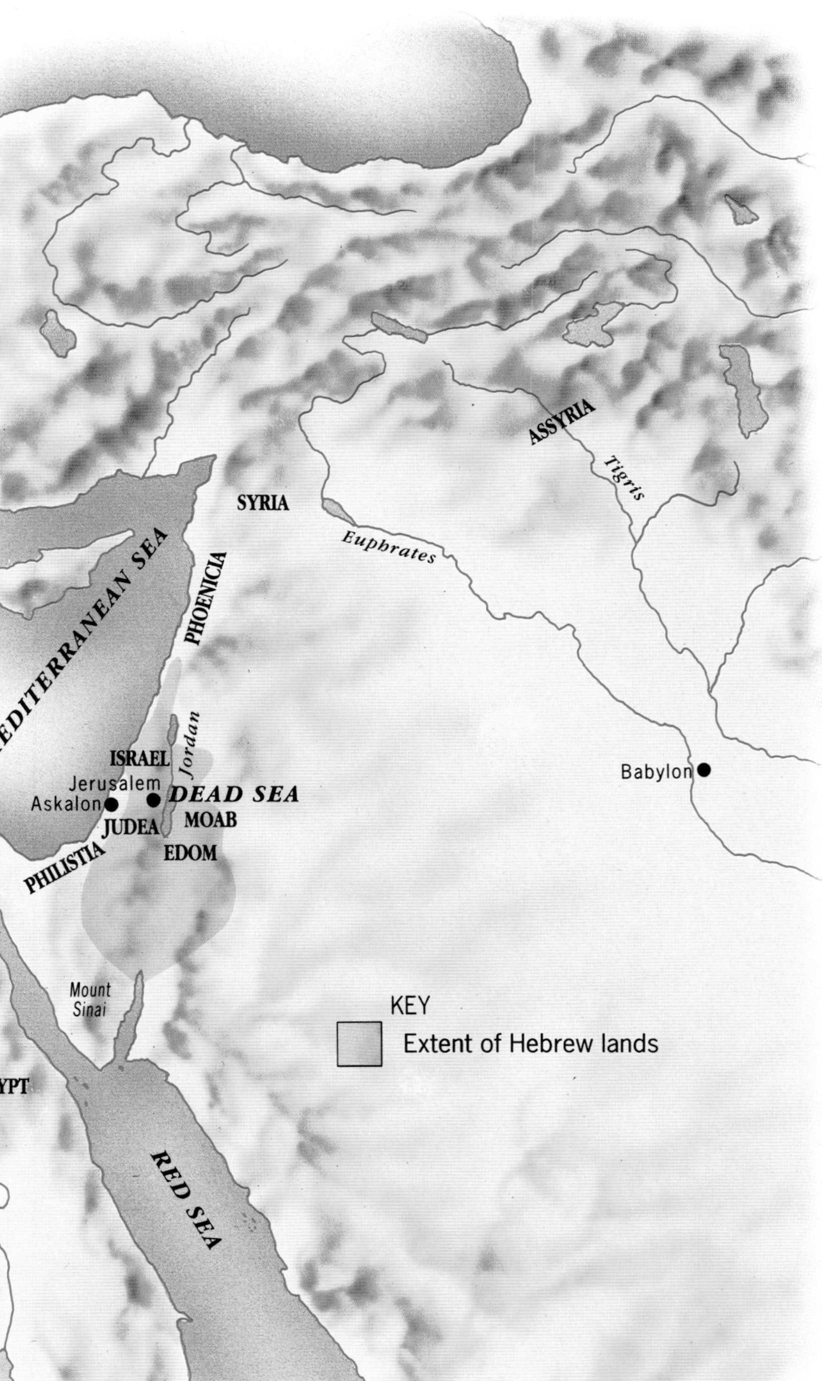

Left Hebrew lands were at the heart of the ancient world. They occupied a tiny area compared to the neighboring empires, which often dominated them. The Hebrew culture was strong enough to survive these pressures.

Above Masada, near the Dead Sea, was the site of a hilltop fort and a palace of King Herod. A Jewish sect called the Zealots made a last stand here against the Romans. In AD 73, after a two-year siege, all 970 of them committed suicide rather than surrender.

The Diaspora

The Arch of Titus in the Forum of Rome was built to celebrate the reconquest of Jerusalem in AD 70 by the future Emperor Titus (reigned AD 79-81).

It was a triumph for the Romans, but a catastrophe for the Jews. From this time on, the Jews began to leave their homeland to settle in other Mediterranean countries and in Western Europe, creating what is called the Diaspora—the dispersion of the Jews outside Israel. They were frequently persecuted. The persecution was most extreme during the Second World War (1939-1945) when the German Nazis attempted to eradicate the Jewish race in what is known as the Holocaust.

THE PERSIANS

The Persians, together with the Medes, nomadic tribes from the Caucasus, had settled into the northern territories of the Assyrian Empire (see pages 22-23) by the 7th century BC. Cyrus the Great, who died in 529 BC, founded the Persian Achaemenid Empire by conquering Media and Lydia between 559 and 547 BC. He went on to take Babylon in 539 BC (see pages 20-21). His son Cambyses conquered Egypt in 525 BC. Darius I (reigned 521-486 BC) extended the empire east as far as the Indus River and Afghanistan, and west to the threshold of Europe.

The Persian Empire was divided into *satrapies* (provinces), and messengers traveled among them quickly on a system of new roads. The Persians were tolerant of local customs and religions, and their own culture was a mixture of elements borrowed from the Assyrians, Babylonians, and Egyptians. The religion of the Persian kings was based on the teachings of Zoroaster (11th century BC). A central idea was the clash between good and evil, in which good will eventually win—a theme echoed later in Christianity.

In the Persian Wars (500-449 BC) the Greeks turned back Persia's advances. The Achaemenid Dynasty was destroyed by Alexander the Great in 331 BC during the reign of Darius III. After Alexander's death, the Seleucids, a dynasty founded by Seleucus, one of Alexander's generals, took over most of the empire and introduced Hellenistic culture. A new and splendid Persian Empire emerged around AD 226 under the Sassanians and lasted until AD 637 when it fell to the Arabs.

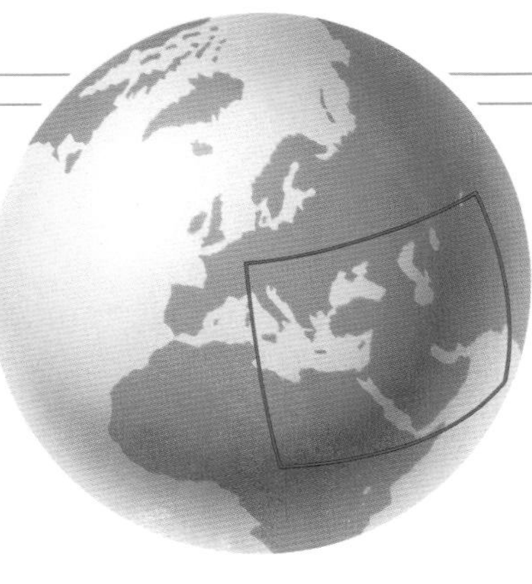

Above The Persian Empire was forged by a highly effective army.This included archers, as depicted in the beautiful glazed tiles from the royal palace at Susa, the old capital of Cyrus the Great.

Above This superb gold model, dating from the 5th century BC, provides detailed information about the construction of a Persian chariot, another important element in the Persian war machine.

City of the Persians

A ceremonial center for the Persian Empire was founded by Darius I at Parsai—now called Persepolis, the Greek name meaning "City of the Persians." It was the setting for the all-important New Year's Festival. Built on a huge stone terrace, it included the palace and treasury, the great audience hall (the Apadana), and the Hall of 100 Columns. The city was built to such an ambitious plan that it was still not complete when it was destroyed by Alexander the Great in 331 BC.

Above Hundreds of ambassadors from all the states within the Persian Empire came to Persepolis to bring tribute to the king. These ceremonies are depicted in stone on the city walls.

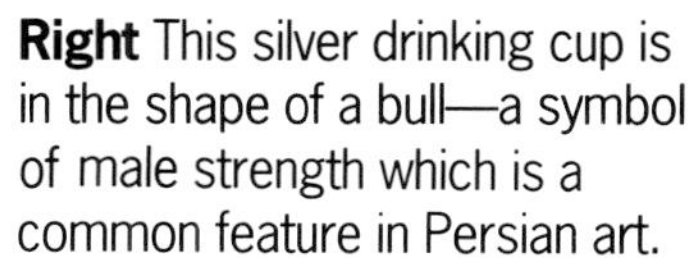

Right This silver drinking cup is in the shape of a bull—a symbol of male strength which is a common feature in Persian art.

Above The tombs of the later kings were built in Persepolis itself, but those of earlier kings were carved into a cliff face at Naqsh-i-Rustam, 3 miles (5 km) to the north of the city. This is the tomb of Darius II, who died in 404 BC.

Below By 500 BC the Persian Achaemenid Empire occupied the lands of all the previous empires of West Asia—including Mesopotamia and Egypt. It was the largest in the world until Alexander the Great incorporated it into his empire.

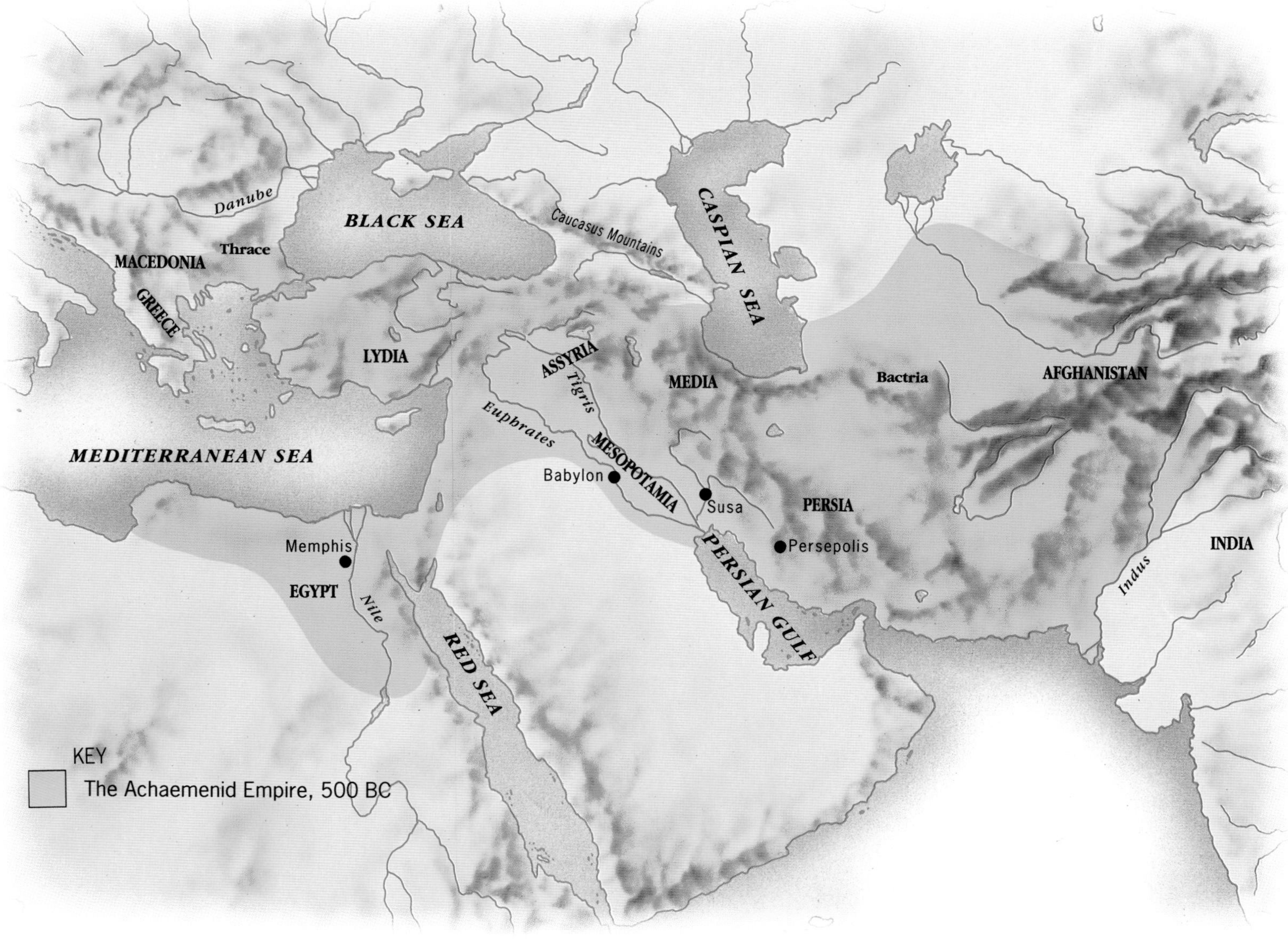

KEY
The Achaemenid Empire, 500 BC

THE ISLAMIC EMPIRE

In the 7th century AD a new force surged through the lands once occupied by the world's first civilizations. This force was Islam, a religion revealed to its Prophet Muhammad (about AD 570-632).

Islam spread from its source in the cities of Mecca and Medina with remarkable speed. By AD 750 the Islamic Empire stretched from the Indus Valley to Spain. Its rulers, successors to Muhammad, were called caliphs.

The Umayyad Caliphate (AD 661-750) was based in Damascus. The Abbasid Caliphate (AD 750-1258) ruled from Baghdad, but by this time the empire had split into a number of independent caliphates.

Islam claimed the same ancestry as Judaism and Christianity and, to begin with, was tolerant of rival religions. Christian and Jewish scholars, poets, and scientists flourished alongside Muslims. In their art and architecture the Islamic rulers were at first content to adopt styles from their new territories—principally those of the Byzantines and the Sassanians. But later a distinctive Islamic style developed.

In the 13th century the Islamic Empire, already weakened by squabbling among its rulers, was unable to fend off the onslaught of the Mongols (see pages 74-75), who sacked Baghdad in 1258. But the Muslim Ottoman Empire (see pages 34-35) soon rose to fill the vacuum in the eastern Mediterranean.

Above The founders of Islam believed that no images of people or animals should distract the faithful from God. So artistic decoration usually takes the form of written religious inscriptions or patterns.

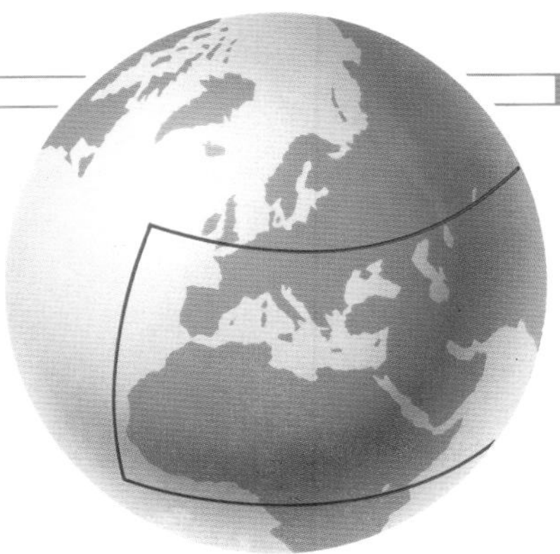

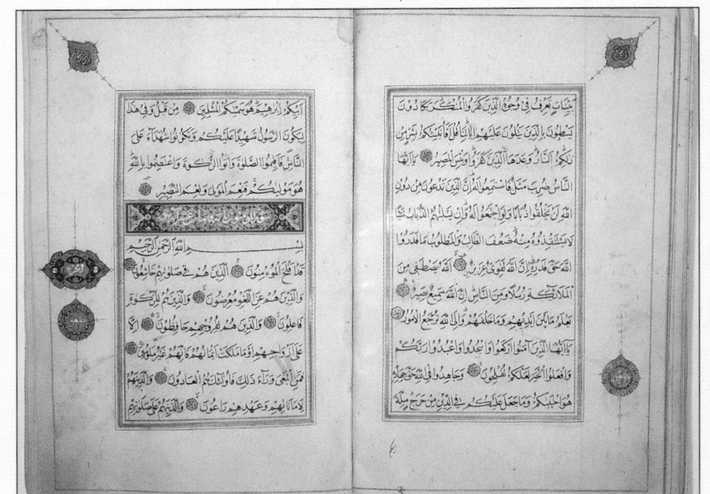

The word of God

The Koran is the holy book of Islam. Muslims believe that it is not simply a text about the religion, but the actual word of God, as revealed by the Angel Gabriel to Muhammad over a period of 20 years. It was first written down several years after Muhammad's death in AD 632.

The Koran deals with the role of God as Creator, the vital need to obey him, and his relationship with Muhammad. It also outlines rules concerning the family, marriage, and other social issues, which form the basis of Islamic law.

The Koran is written in a very beautiful style of Arabic, which is suitable for chanting. The sacred text demands the greatest skills of Arabic calligraphers—scribes who treat the written word as an art form.

Left According to the "Five Pillars of Islam" —the basic rules of the faith—all Muslims should go on pilgrimage to Mecca at least once. For centuries, thousands of pilgrims have traveled to Mecca for the annual pilgrimage, called the *Hajj*. As part of the tradition, pilgrims circle the cube-shaped building called the *Kaaba*. This is Islam's holiest shrine, and is said to be the site of the first mosque, built by Abraham.

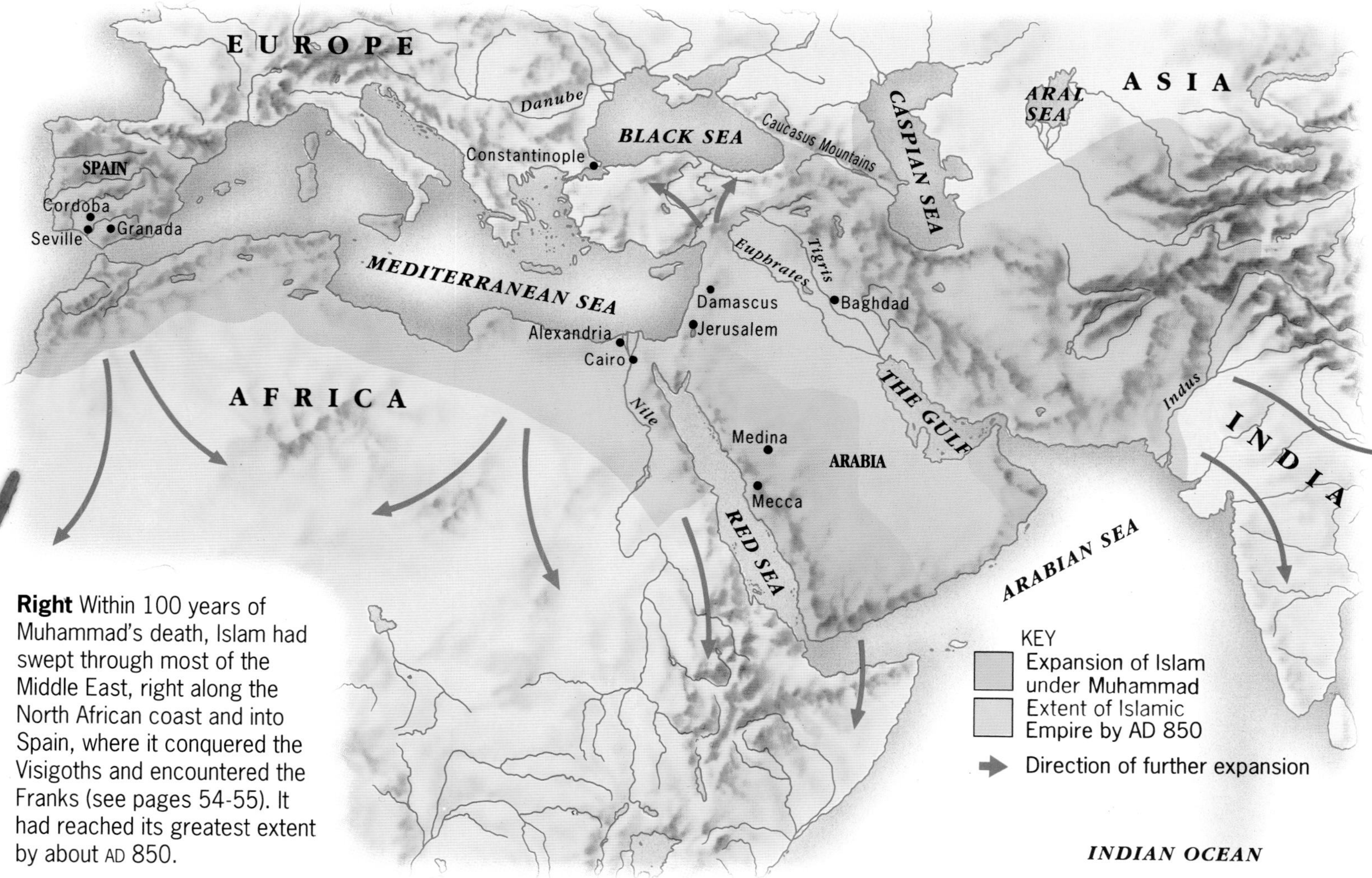

EUROPE
ASIA
ARAL SEA
Danube
BLACK SEA
Caucasus Mountains
CASPIAN SEA
SPAIN
Cordoba
Granada
Seville
Constantinople
MEDITERRANEAN SEA
Euphrates
Tigris
Damascus
Baghdad
Jerusalem
Alexandria
Cairo
AFRICA
Nile
THE GULF
Indus
INDIA
Medina
ARABIA
Mecca
RED SEA
ARABIAN SEA
INDIAN OCEAN

KEY
Expansion of Islam under Muhammad
Extent of Islamic Empire by AD 850
Direction of further expansion

Right Within 100 years of Muhammad's death, Islam had swept through most of the Middle East, right along the North African coast and into Spain, where it conquered the Visigoths and encountered the Franks (see pages 54-55). It had reached its greatest extent by about AD 850.

Left The Ibn Tulun mosque in Cairo shows the distinctive Islamic style of architecture that was beginning to develop by the 9th century AD. The faithful were called to prayer from the top of the tower, called a minaret.

Below Islam was also spread through trade. Caravans across the Sahara took Islam to West Africa. Arab seafarers took it to the east coast of Africa and to India. By the 13th century it had reached Southeast Asia.

Below The Arabs produced some of the most magnificent Islamic architecture in Spain. This mosque at Cordoba was begun in the 8th century AD. The Moors, as they were known, invaded Spain from North Africa in AD 711 and ruled from several cities there, including Cordoba, Granada, and Seville. They were finally driven out of Spain by the Christian kingdoms in 1492.

THE OTTOMAN EMPIRE

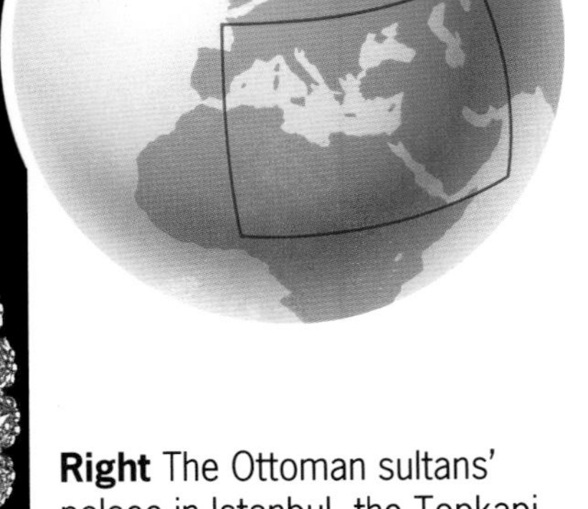

Right The Ottoman sultans' palace in Istanbul, the Topkapi, contains one of the world's richest collections of gems and jewelry, including this huge 86-carat "Spoon Diamond."

The Ottoman Empire was a Muslim empire founded by—and named after—Osman I in the 13th century. For nearly 700 years afterward it was ruled by his descendants.

The empire originated in Turkey, where the Ottomans took over the old Seljuk states, which had been overrun by the Mongols (see pages 74-75). Then they attacked the eastern territories of the Byzantine Empire, expanded into the Balkans and surrounded the city of Constantinople. Further progress in empire-building, however, received a temporary setback in 1402 when the Mongol conqueror Timur defeated Sultan Bayezid I (reigned 1389-1402).

Constantinople was finally captured in 1453 by Mehmet II (reigned 1451-1481), who was called "the Conqueror," but who was also a poet and scholar who spoke six languages. Constantinople was renamed Istanbul and became the Ottoman capital.

By the end of the 15th century the Ottomans had conquered much of the Balkans. The Ottoman Empire reached its full extent under Selim I (reigned 1512-1520) and his son Suleiman ("the Magnificent," reigned 1520-1566). Selim I took over the caliphate, and from then on the Ottoman rulers claimed to be the spiritual rulers of Islam (see pages 32-33). However, they were generally tolerant of other religions within their empire.

The empire now included much of eastern Europe, western Asia, and northern Africa, and the Ottoman fleet under Admiral Khayr ad-Din, known as Barbarossa (about 1466-1546), dominated the Mediterranean. Decline set in after Suleiman's death, however. Disputes among the Ottoman rulers gave increasing control to the viziers (chief ministers) and the elite troops called the janissaries. During the 18th century the empire began to disintegrate, but it finally came to an end only after the First World War, in 1923.

Magnificent ruler

Under Suleiman I, the Ottoman Empire had its "Golden Age." He conquered Mesopotamia, took almost the entire North African coast, defeated the Hungarians at the Battle of Mohacs in 1526, and laid siege to Vienna—unsuccessfully—in 1529. Despite this, he is said to have detested war.

Suleiman ruled over an immensely wealthy empire of 14 million people. England at this time, under Henry VIII, had just 2.5 million people. Suleiman was called "the Magnificent" by the French, who were his allies. But he became famous throughout Europe for the elegance of Istanbul, the splendor of the new public buildings and mosques, and his passion for the spectacular pageants and ceremonies that he arranged for state occasions. He was the first sultan to move his court permanently to the Topkapi palace.

To his own people Suleiman was known as "the Law Giver," mainly for his reforms of laws about the ownership of land. He reformed education and introduced important changes to the administration of the empire, which gave greater powers to the provincial governors, who were called *pashas.*

Above The Ottomans converted the magnificent Byzantine church of Hagia Sophia in Istanbul to a mosque (see pages 52-53). In 1619 Sultan Ahmet built a mosque to a very similar plan close by (above). It is known as the Blue Mosque because the interior is covered with over 20,000 beautiful blue patterned tiles.

Janissaries

The janissaries were highly-trained infantrymen. They formed part of the sultan's personal household and wore a distinctive cap.

Above Under Sultan Selim II (reigned 1566-1574) the Ottomans tried to extend their empire in Europe by attacking the territories of the Venetian Republic in the Adriatic Sea. In 1571 Venice joined forces with Spain and defeated the Ottoman fleet at the Battle of Lepanto, in western Greece.

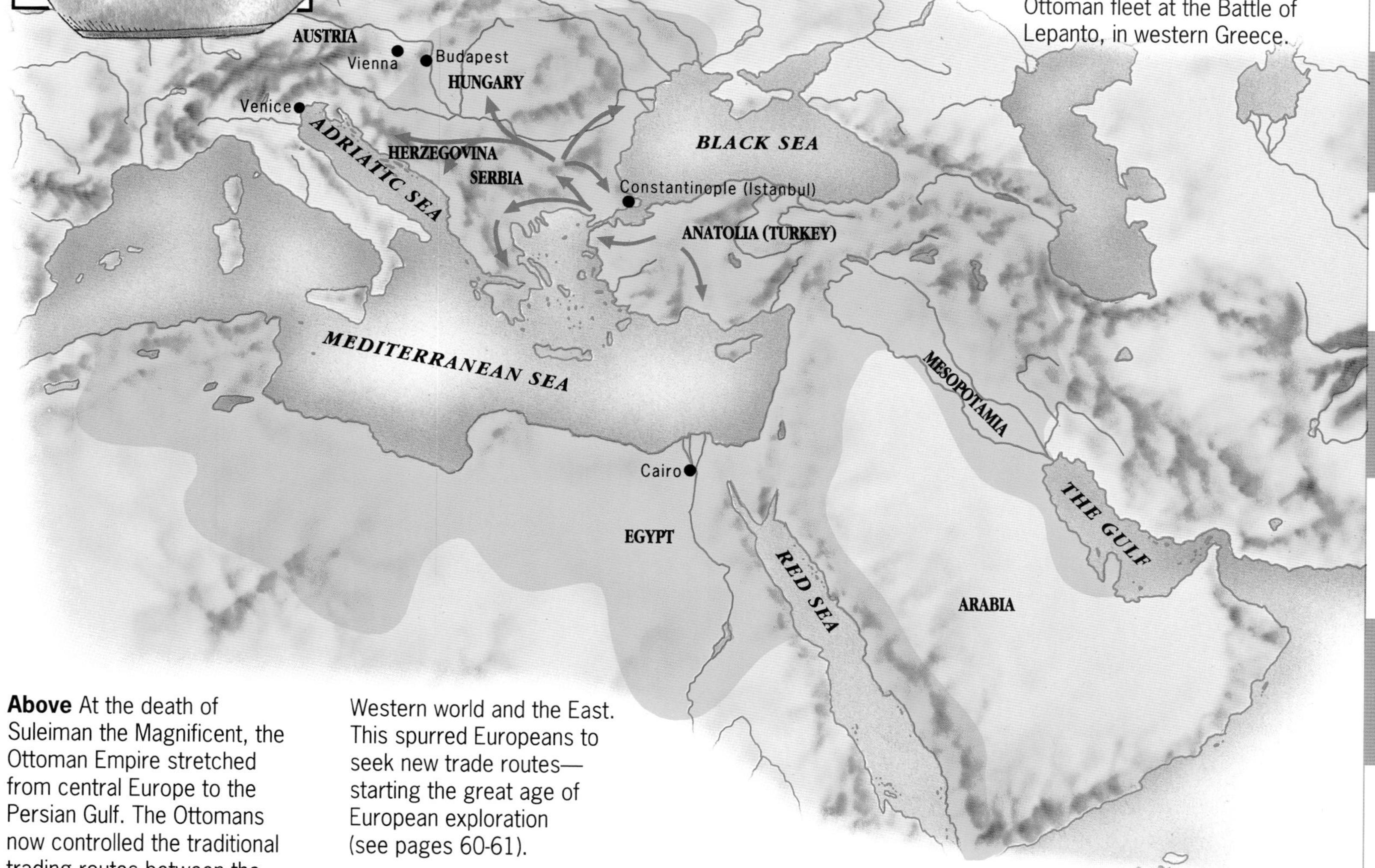

KEY

Ottoman Empire in 1520 under Selim I

Main routes of Ottoman conquest

Above At the death of Suleiman the Magnificent, the Ottoman Empire stretched from central Europe to the Persian Gulf. The Ottomans now controlled the traditional trading routes between the Western world and the East. This spurred Europeans to seek new trade routes—starting the great age of European exploration (see pages 60-61).

SECTION 5: EUROPE

Much of Europe was still in the Stone Age when the pyramids were built. But civilization caught hold in the northern Mediterranean, and was carried farther north by the Romans. Then, after a thousand years of turmoil, the Europeans rediscovered the ancient world.

Above The Castlerigg stone circle in Cumbria, England, is one of numerous megalithic monuments found in Europe. The stones of such circles are usually aligned according to astronomical observations, suggesting that they were used for religious ceremonies at specific times of the year.

Beaker people

The tools of the late Neolithic period and early Bronze Age may have been simple, but beautiful craftwork was produced. The Beaker people are named for the beakerlike pots that have been found in early Bronze Age burial sites in much of central and western Europe. Their pottery was handmade, without the help of a wheel, and fired at a low temperature. But its decoration shows a delicate touch, and an appreciation of beauty in its skillful use of patterning.

NEOLITHIC AND BRONZE AGE EUROPE

An important change took place in Europe when people first began to practice farming and create settled communities. This was the dawn of the New Stone Age, or Neolithic period (*lithos* means stone in Greek)—as opposed to the Old Stone Age (Palaeolithic) which had preceded it. Tools were still made of polished stone and flint, but were now used to help in the work of growing grain, making flour, and raising farm animals.

A more settled village life encouraged the development of pottery and weaving. Although people lived in small villages, they could cooperate successfully in large numbers to undertake major projects such as building monuments and tombs.

The Neolithic period in Europe took place roughly between 4000 and 2400 BC. The next phase occurred when Europeans started to use metals instead of stone and flint to make weapons and tools. Bronze casting had been developed in the Middle East by about 3500 BC, and the use of bronze was well established in Europe by 2000 BC.

The Bronze Age was replaced by the Iron Age as knowledge about iron-working techniques spread through southern Europe after 1200 BC.

Respect for the dead

While the ancient Egyptians were carrying out their elaborate rituals for burying the dead, the Neolithic people of northern Europe were building their own ambitious tombs. One of the largest and most complete is at Newgrange, in Ireland (above). This is a "passage tomb," built in around 3000 BC, and so called because bodies were placed in a chamber at the end of a long passage. The entrance is marked by a decorative feature—a stone carved with intricate spiral patterns. The whole of the tomb was covered in a mound of earth 300 ft (92 m) across.

The Bronze Age

Copper was the first metal to be widely used in Europe, from around 3000 BC. It was produced by smelting—heating copper ore at a high temperature. The metal was then made into shapes by casting it in molds and

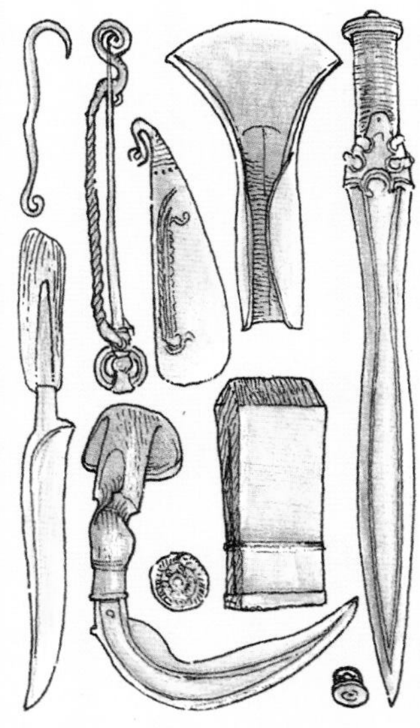

hammering it. Copper is a soft metal, but when it is mixed with tin it becomes a much harder metal called bronze. When bronze was discovered, metals could be used to make stronger, more effective weapons and tools.

KEY

Areas where megalithic tombs have been found

Centers of bronze working

Main tin sources

Expansion of agriculture

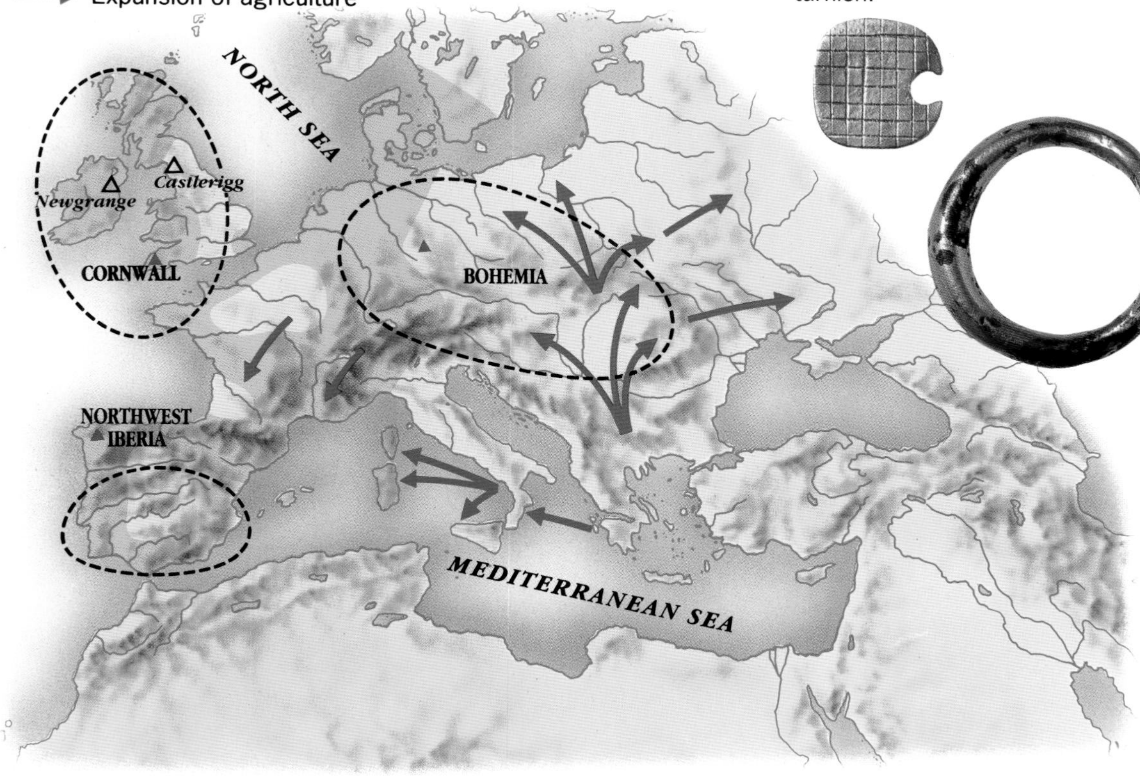

NORTH SEA

Newgrange

Castlerigg

CORNWALL

BOHEMIA

NORTHWEST IBERIA

MEDITERRANEAN SEA

Below Early metalworkers also discovered gold. It is a soft metal, ideal for jewelry and ornaments because it is fairly easy to work. Also, it does not tarnish.

Left In many parts of the eastern Mediterranean evidence of Neolithic and early Bronze Age civilization has been found. Innovations in settled farming filtered slowly northward, taking 1,000 years or more to cross the continent. Metalworking probably developed separately in Europe.

THE MINOANS AND MYCENAEANS

After about 2200 BC the Bronze Age Minoans (see box below) developed a highly distinctive culture on the island of Crete. They grew rich from the fertile farmland of the island, and also from sea trade, including trade with ancient Egypt (see pages 14-15). Palaces were built at Knossos, Phaistos, Mallia, and Zakro. Minoan influence also spread to neighboring islands, notably Santorin (then called Thera). This volcanic island erupted around 1500-1450 BC, smothering the Minoan communities there, and possibly causing the decline of the whole Minoan civilization—all the palaces in Crete were destroyed at about this time.

The focus of northern Mediterranean civilization then moved to the Greek mainland. The Mycenaeans first appeared in this region around 2000 BC and developed contacts with Minoans. They are named after the ancient city of Mycenae, but had other centers of power, including Tiryns, Pylos, and Athens. By 1600 BC they were vying with the Minoans for supremacy, and may have invaded Crete. From around 1450 to 1100 BC they were the main power in the region.

These civilizations were known only through Greek myths until the 19th century, when the work of archaeologists showed that the myths were based on historical fact. The Minoans used a form of hieroglyphics called Linear A, which has still not been deciphered. The Mycenaeans' Linear B script, however, has been deciphered.

Below The Minoan deities were connected with the forces of nature and fertility, and were worshipped in caves and other natural sites in prehistoric times. This pottery model of a snake goddess, or a snake priestess, was found in the central shrine of the palace of Knossos. Snakes were both feared and revered: they were thought to become young again each time they shed their skin. Associated with healing, the snake still forms part of the symbol of the medical profession.

City of the Minotaur

At its height, the Minoan palace of Knossos and the town around it housed many thousands of people. The huge royal palace, which was the center of power, was probably first built around 1970 BC. It consisted of a series of flat-roofed buildings, some several storys high, set around a large courtyard. Excavations, begun in 1899 under the direction of the British archaeologist Sir Arthur Evans (1851-1941), revealed grand apartments, many of them decorated with superb wall paintings, and an extensive range of storerooms. The palace was said to have been built by the semi-legendary King Minos, after whom Evans named the civilization. According to traditional legend, Minos kept a mythical bull-headed beast called the Minotaur in a labyrinth beneath the palace. Certainly the bull was a sacred symbol of the Minoans, and paintings in the palace depict acrobats somersaulting over bulls—perhaps as part of some kind of religious festival.

The mask of death

This superb gold death mask was discovered by the German archaeologist Heinrich Schliemann (1822-1890) at the royal grave site of the city of Mycenae. He thought the grave might belong to Agamemnon, the Mycenaean king who, according to the Greek poet Homer, led the Greeks against Troy in the 1200s BC. In fact the graves were older than this, dating back to about 1600 BC. The grave site formed part of the citadel of Mycenae, which included a palace. Mycenaean palaces in general were heavily fortified, but rather less grand than Minoan ones. Linear B tablets tell us that the Mycenaean kings controlled extensive farmlands worked by large numbers of slaves, as well as workshops that produced metals and pottery.

Above The Minoans are famous for their charming and striking wall paintings or frescoes. This picture of a boy carrying fishes comes from Thera.

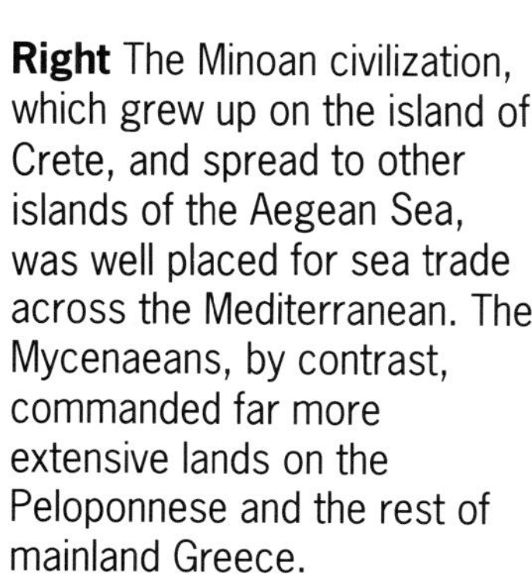

Left Mycenaean pottery shows the vital part the sea played in people's lives.

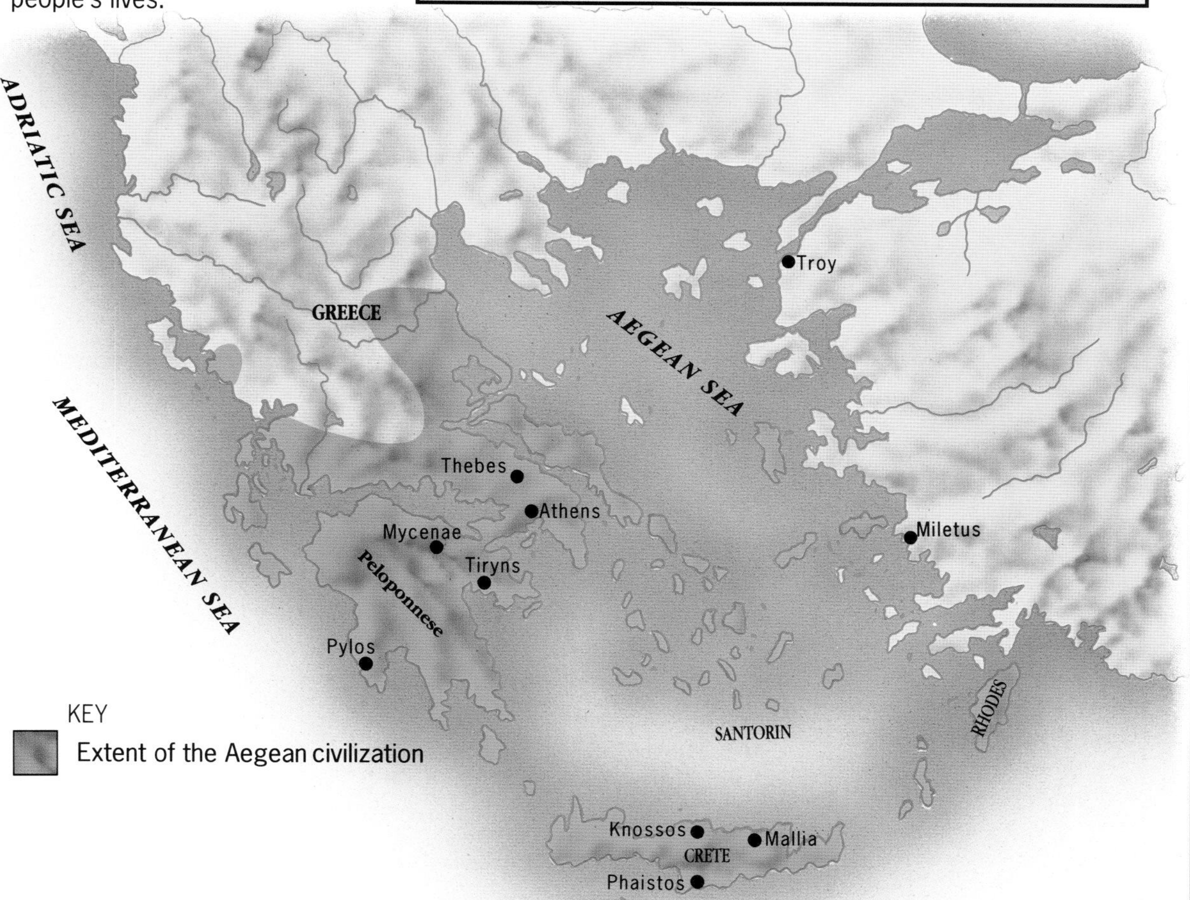

Right The Minoan civilization, which grew up on the island of Crete, and spread to other islands of the Aegean Sea, was well placed for sea trade across the Mediterranean. The Mycenaeans, by contrast, commanded far more extensive lands on the Peloponnese and the rest of mainland Greece.

ANCIENT GREECE

By about 1400 BC the Mycenaeans had established trading posts around the Eastern Mediterranean. After a period of turmoil following the collapse of the Mycenaean cities, Greece entered the Dark Ages, a time when civilization and learning progressed slowly. Then numerous city-states began to develop again. They acted more or less independently and practiced every kind of government, from tyranny to democracy.

During the so-called Archaic Period (about 800-500 BC), the Greeks began to show their unusual talents in the arts, notably in sculpture and in their pottery, which was stylishly decorated with black figures. Trade took the Greeks across the Mediterranean, and after the 8th century BC they began to create colonies abroad, such as Magna Graecia in southern Italy.

The Persians (see pages 30-31) attempted to invade Greece, but were defeated in the Persian Wars (500-450 BC), when the cities joined forces, led by Athens and Sparta. What followed is called the Golden Age of Greek culture. A period of great prosperity was accompanied by advances in philosophy, mathematics, astronomy, medicine, literature, art, and architecture. Much of the Greek learning which developed remained unmatched in Europe until it was rediscovered during the Renaissance 2,000 years later.

Under the leadership of Pericles (about 495-429 BC) Athens flourished and a system of democratic government evolved. But rivalry with other city-states led to the brutal Peloponnesian War (431-404 BC) and the conquest of Athens by Sparta. The Macedonians (see pages 42-43) conquered Greece in 338 BC, and when the Romans took over from the Macedonians in 146 BC, Greece became a part of the Roman Empire.

Left This statue shows the shield, helmet, and body armor of a hoplite, the infantryman of the Greek army.

Below Greek sculpture was more realistic than that of any previous civilization. This clay statue of the 5th century BC shows two women playing a game of knuckle-bones, or jacks.

Fathers of modern theater

The Greeks laid the foundations of European theatrical tradition and built spectacular theaters. The tiered banks of stone seats gave an excellent view for up to 15,000 people. The acoustics were good enough to carry the smallest sound to the back of the audience.

Perfect proportions

At the end of the Persian Wars, Pericles persuaded the people of Athens to build a temple to give thanks to their patron goddess, Athena, and to memorialize their dead. The Parthenon was built on the Acropolis, a rocky hill that dominates the city. The main architect was the sculptor Phidias, who created a huge sculpture of Athena, made of ivory and a ton of gold, to place inside.

The Parthenon was a monument of perfect proportions. It was built of white marble from the quarries of Mount Pentelicon, 10 miles (16 km) from Athens, and marble sculptures lined the outside, and adorned both ends. The building took just 15 years to complete—a remarkably short time for the period—and it was finished in 432 BC.

After about AD 500 the Parthenon was used as a Christian church, then as a mosque. In 1687 the Parthenon became a store for gunpowder, and exploded when the Venetians bombarded it. Even after nearly 1,500 years of neglect, however, it is still clear why this became one of the most admired buildings of the ancient world.

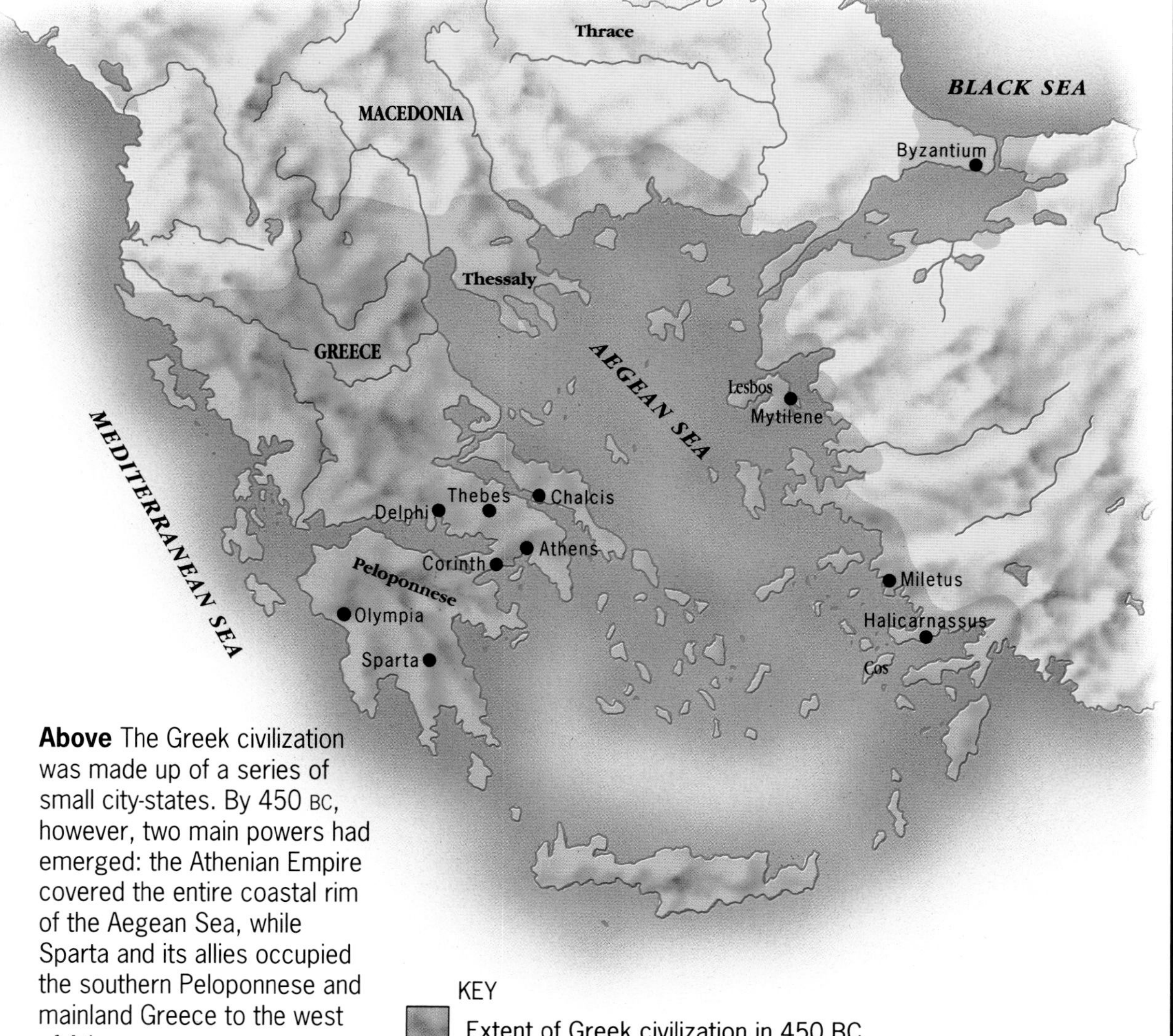

Above The Greek civilization was made up of a series of small city-states. By 450 BC, however, two main powers had emerged: the Athenian Empire covered the entire coastal rim of the Aegean Sea, while Sparta and its allies occupied the southern Peloponnese and mainland Greece to the west of Athens.

First coins

In early civilizations traders bartered their goods, exchanging one item for another, such as a sheep for a hammer. Later, pieces of precious metal were used to pay for things. These were stamped with the emblem of the city or the image of a god, to guarantee their value, and became the first coins.

The Greeks borrowed the idea of coins from the Lydians. One of their coins was the talent, originally a Persian measure. Over time their coins became more and more sophisticated.This made them objects of beauty, and also helped to prevent forgery.

THE MACEDONIANS

Macedon was an independent state of ancient Greece, generally looked down on by the Greek cities for its lack of culture. However, King Philip II of Macedon (reigned 359-336 BC) created a powerful army and in 338 BC he defeated Athens and Thebes at the Battle of Chaeronea to become master of all Greece. He now prepared to invade the Persian Empire (see pages 30-31), but was murdered by a member of his bodyguard.

Philip's place was taken by Alexander III, his son, now known as Alexander the Great (reigned 336-323 BC). In 334 BC he defeated the Persians at Granicus, then conquered Tyre in Phoenicia before taking Egypt, where he was made pharaoh. Alexander's dream was to create a multi-racial Greek-Persian empire, and he encouraged many of his men to marry Persian women. He himself married a Persian princess named Roxane. He pushed on eastward, but after reaching the Indus Valley in 326 BC, his exhausted troops persuaded him to turn back. Alexander died of fever in Babylon in 323 BC; he was only 33 years old.

Alexander's empire spread Greek (or Hellenistic) culture throughout the eastern Mediterranean and western Asia. Dynasties founded by Macedonian generals (the Seleucids) in Asia Minor, Mesopotamia, and Persia and the Ptolemies in Egypt ruled for over two centuries. However, the empire was weakened by division and dispute. Macedon itself was defeated by Rome and became a Roman province in 146 BC.

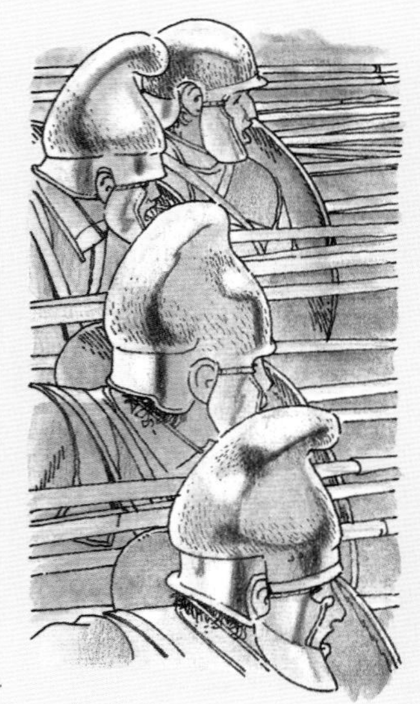

Into battle

Macedonian soldiers wore light body-armor as well as helmets. They were well known for using a battle formation called the phalanx. Tightly-packed ranks of soldiers, holding long spears and shields, fended off the enemy while the cavalry attacked from the side.

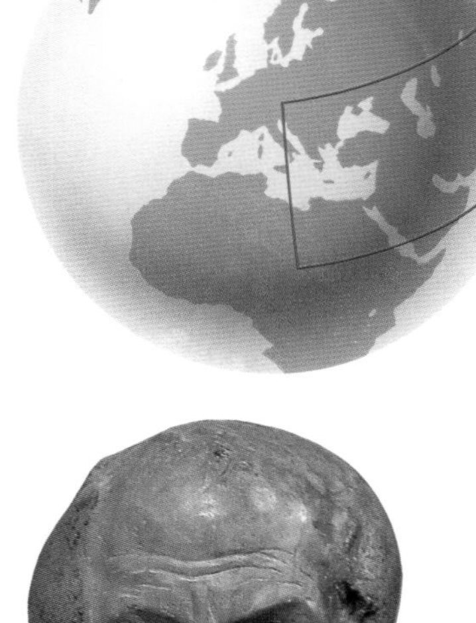

Above Among Alexander's teachers was the great Greek philosopher Aristotle (384-322 BC), whose father had been a doctor to one of the kings of Macedon. Philip II invited Aristotle to Macedon after his conquest of Greece.

Macedonian might

Alexander fought and won three major battles with the Persians, who were led by Darius III, at Granicus (334 BC), Issus (333 BC), and Gaugamela (331 BC). The Battle of Issus is the subject of a mosaic (left) of the 2nd or 1st century BC, found at the Roman city of Pompeii. Alexander is on the left, on his famous horse, Bucephalus. Darius is in the center, in a chariot. At Gaugamela, Alexander is said to have had only 47,000 troops, while the Persian army numbered a million.

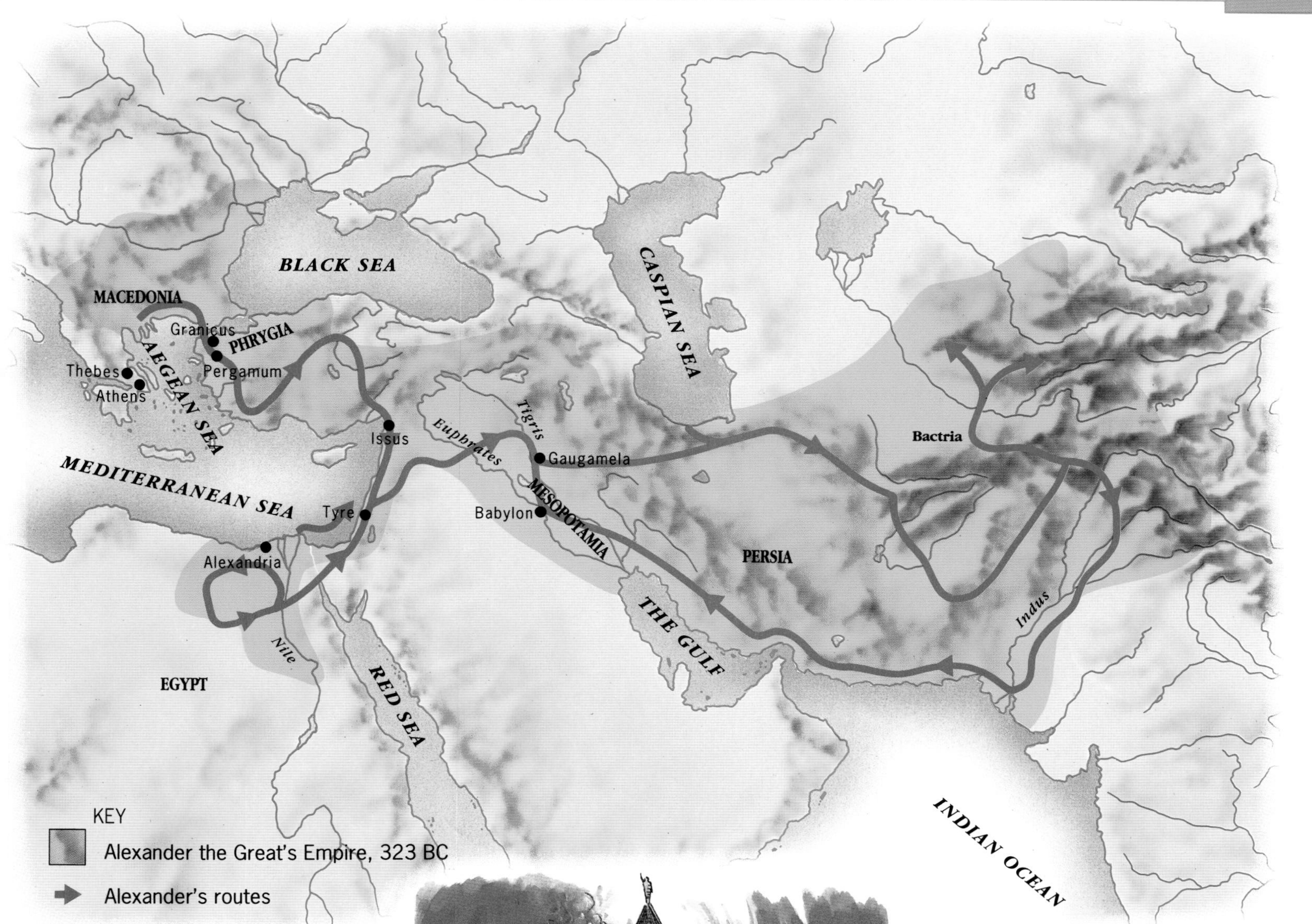

MACEDONIA
BLACK SEA
CASPIAN SEA
Granicus
PHRYGIA
AEGEAN SEA
Thebes
Athens
Pergamum
Issus
Euphrates
Tigris
Gaugamela
Bactria
MEDITERRANEAN SEA
Tyre
Babylon
MESOPOTAMIA
PERSIA
Alexandria
THE GULF
Indus
Nile
EGYPT
RED SEA
INDIAN OCEAN

KEY
Alexander the Great's Empire, 323 BC
Alexander's routes

Above The Empire of Alexander the Great was the largest of the ancient world, stretching from Greece to the Indus Valley, and including Mesopotamia and Egypt. It is estimated that Alexander himself traveled 20,000 miles during the 11 years of his conquests.

Beacon of learning

Alexander founded some 70 cities, including Alexandria on the Mediterranean coast of Egypt. After his death one of his generals, Ptolemy, took Alexander's body to Egypt, hoping that it would give him mystical power. It was later buried in Alexandria, which became the capital of Egypt during the rule of the Ptolemaic Dynasty, and one of the great cities of the Mediterranean.

The Pharos lighthouse was built about 280 BC. It was the first of its kind, and one of the Seven Wonders of the Ancient World.

Alexandria also had a famous library, containing 700,000 books, and remained an important center of learning for about 600 years.

Right Pergamum was an Ancient Greek city-state that ruled an empire in Asia Minor from around 190 to 133 BC, when it was taken over by the Romans. It was a wealthy trading city and a center of Hellenistic culture. Its name gave rise to the word "parchment," the thin sheets of animal skin which, after the 2nd century BC, were used as a writing material instead of papyrus.

Above Ptolemy III (reigned 246-221 BC) was the grandson of the founder of the Macedonian Dynasty that ruled Egypt for 274 years. Ptolemaic Egypt came to a close in 30 BC when it became part of the Roman Empire.

THE ETRUSCANS

The Etruscans had settled in western central Italy by about the 12th century BC. Just where they came from no one knows. They spoke their own distinct language, which appears to have no connection with any other.

Etruscan culture developed over some 400 years, reaching a peak in the 7th and 6th centuries BC. Etruria was never a single, united country, but a confederation of independent city-states, such as Tavxuna (called Tarquinia today), Veii (Veio), Volterra, Volsinii (Orvieto), Perusia (Perugia), and Clusium (Chiusi). The Etruscans were successful traders and noted seafarers. They had contacts with Carthage and Greece, and their own colonies in Corsica, Sardinia, and Elba. They were also gifted engineers, foreshadowing the Romans with their roads, bridges, sewage systems, and aqueducts.

Their culture began to decline in the 5th century BC when they were harassed by the Celts (see pages 48-49) and forced to withdraw from their northern territories around the Po Valley. There is evidence that Etruscans were involved in the early history of Rome. As Rome's power increased, some Etruscan towns became Roman allies, while others resisted. Veii was conquered in 396 BC, and Volsinii in 264 BC. Gradually Etruria was absorbed into the Roman Empire, but Etruscan was still spoken in the 1st century BC.

Above The quality of Etruscan craftsmanship is displayed in this embossed gold bulla, a kind of medallion worn around the neck.

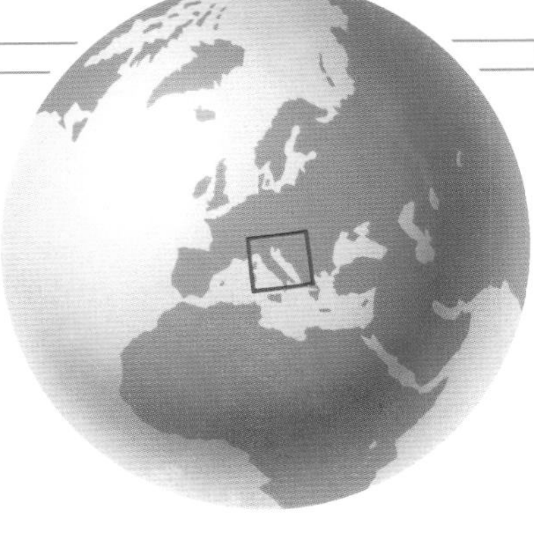

Below The Etruscans excelled in bronze-work. This cover for a storage jar is typical of the way they decorated even everyday objects with lively, imaginative, and witty figures.

Alive in death

One of the great finds from the Etruscan civilization is this sarcophagus, or coffin, for a couple from Caere (called Ceveteri today), near Rome. It was made of terracotta (baked clay) in the 6th century BC. The couple look relaxed, affectionate, and very much alive. The sculpture seems to suggest that women had equal importance in Etruscan life—unlike in the Greek and Roman worlds, which were dominated by men.

The manufacture of such a large piece of pottery required considerable skill. But the Etruscans were master potters. They were famous for their ornately modeled black *bucchero* pottery. In addition they imported Greek pottery, and made Greek-style vases and dishes that were as good as the Greek originals.

Right The Etruscans wanted their dead to have every chance of enjoying the afterlife. They were buried with all kinds of artifacts, treasures, and luxuries, such as pottery and jewelry. Some were also provided with elaborate chambers painted with animals, mythical figures, and joyous scenes of dancing, hunting, music-making, and feasting. These paintings tell us a great deal about Etruscan life. It is possible that Etruscan homes were decorated in a similar way; the dead would therefore feel at home in the afterlife. This tomb, at Tarquinia, dates from the 6th century BC.

Below The Etruscans originally inhabited a region on the coast of western central Italy now called Tuscany (from a Latin version of their name, *Tusci*). Their territory later extended farther south, beyond Rome, and north to the valley of the Po River.

Right The arched gateway to the town of Volterra is a remnant of the Etruscan city walls, and is still in use after 2,000 years.

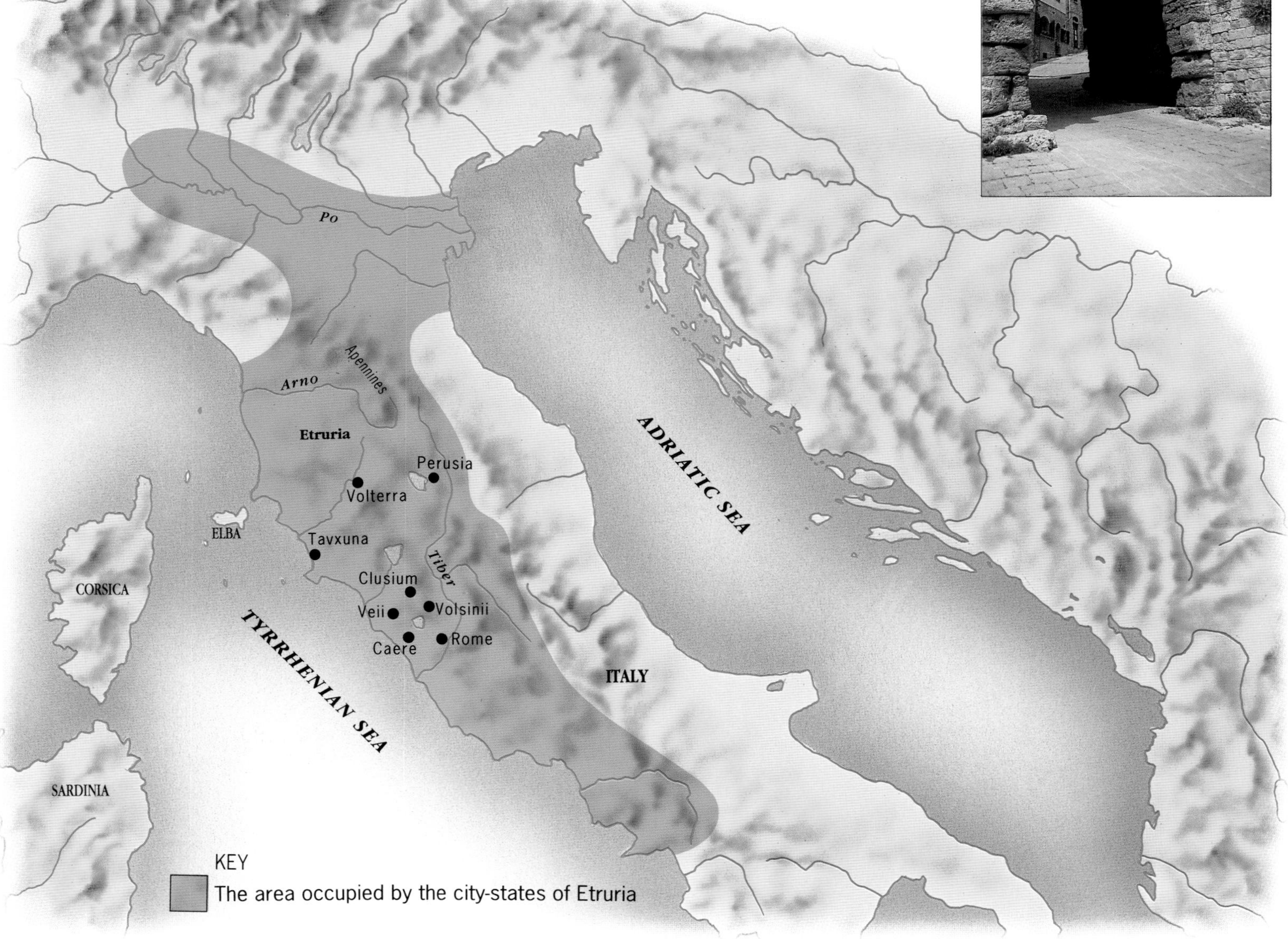

KEY

The area occupied by the city-states of Etruria

THE ROMANS

The Romans created the most advanced European civilization of ancient times. After the collapse of the Roman Empire it took the European nations about a thousand years before they could begin to match its skills in engineering, town planning, architecture, science, medicine, and literature. The Romans, in their turn, owed much of their knowledge and understanding of the world to the ancient Greeks.

Some of the early kings of Rome were Etruscans. They reigned for about 250 years until they were overthrown and replaced by the Roman Republic. Rome was then ruled by a government of 300 or more senators.

Rome began to spread its influence over the whole Italian peninsula. By defeating Carthage in the three Punic Wars (264-146 BC), it took control of the Mediterranean.

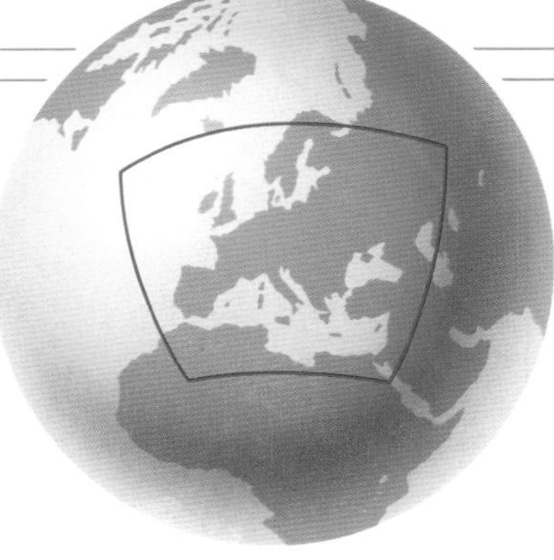

Left This necklace was found at Pompeii. The delicate gold chain work contrasts with the rugged mother-of-pearl and green stones.

Julius Caesar (100-44 BC), the greatest of Roman leaders, extended the territory in western Europe during a troubled period for the republic that ended in civil war. The republic was replaced by the rule of emperors and the Roman Empire found stability. The 2nd century AD was a golden age.

Christianity became an increasingly strong force, even though it was suppressed, sometimes violently, until the reign of Emperor Constantine I (reigned AD 306-37). He moved the capital from Rome to Byzantium. The Western Empire, based on Rome, collapsed under a series of Barbarian invasions (see pages 50-51), but the Eastern Empire survived and evolved into the Byzantine Empire (see pages 52-53).

All roads lead to Rome

The Romans take their name from their capital city, Rome. For over 1,000 years it was at the heart of Roman civilization. According to legend, the city was founded in 753 BC by Romulus; as infants, he and his twin brother Remus were saved from death by drinking the milk of a female wolf. The city was built on seven hills, and the Forum (above) lay in the center, between the Palatine and Capitoline hills. This was the religious and political hub of the city, and a popular meeting place. It contained government buildings, banks, temples to various gods, monuments to Rome's military achievements, and the Via Sacra (sacred way) down which victorious generals would march in triumph.

Left The Romans held their leaders in great respect, and honored them with statues. This marble statue of Augustus (63 BC-AD 14) shows him dressed as a general. Augustus was the great nephew and adopted son of Julius Caesar. He took over power during the turbulent years after Caesar was murdered, and he became the first emperor in 27 BC. The reign of Augustus was a prosperous period, during which the city of Rome was transformed by new buildings. It marked a high point in Roman culture, noted in particular for its literature. Famous authors included Virgil, Horace, Ovid, and Livy.

Left In AD 79 the volcano Vesuvius erupted, pouring choking fumes and tons of ash over Pompeii and Herculaneum, two cities to the south of Naples. Pompeii remained buried for over 1,600 years. Since 1748 it has been excavated bit by bit, revealing a complete (if damaged) Roman city. The so-called Villa of the Mysteries includes a dining room decorated with some of the finest paintings of the Roman world.

Keeping clean

The Romans understood the importance of hygiene and cleanliness, and they also realized that baths were good for relaxation. The city of Bath, in southwestern England, owes its name to its Roman baths (below), which can still be seen today.

Right The civil engineers of the Roman Empire played a major role in town planning: in building design, road construction, and sewage systems. Aqueducts are among the most impressive monuments to Roman achievement. They were part of an elaborate system that transported fresh water to towns from sources many miles away. The Pont du Gard is near the city of Nîmes in southern France.

Below The Roman Empire reached its greatest extent under Emperor Trajan (ruled AD 98-117). By the end of his reign, it stretched all the way around the Mediterranean and Black Sea, through to the Gulf, and covered almost all of Western Europe, including England and Wales.

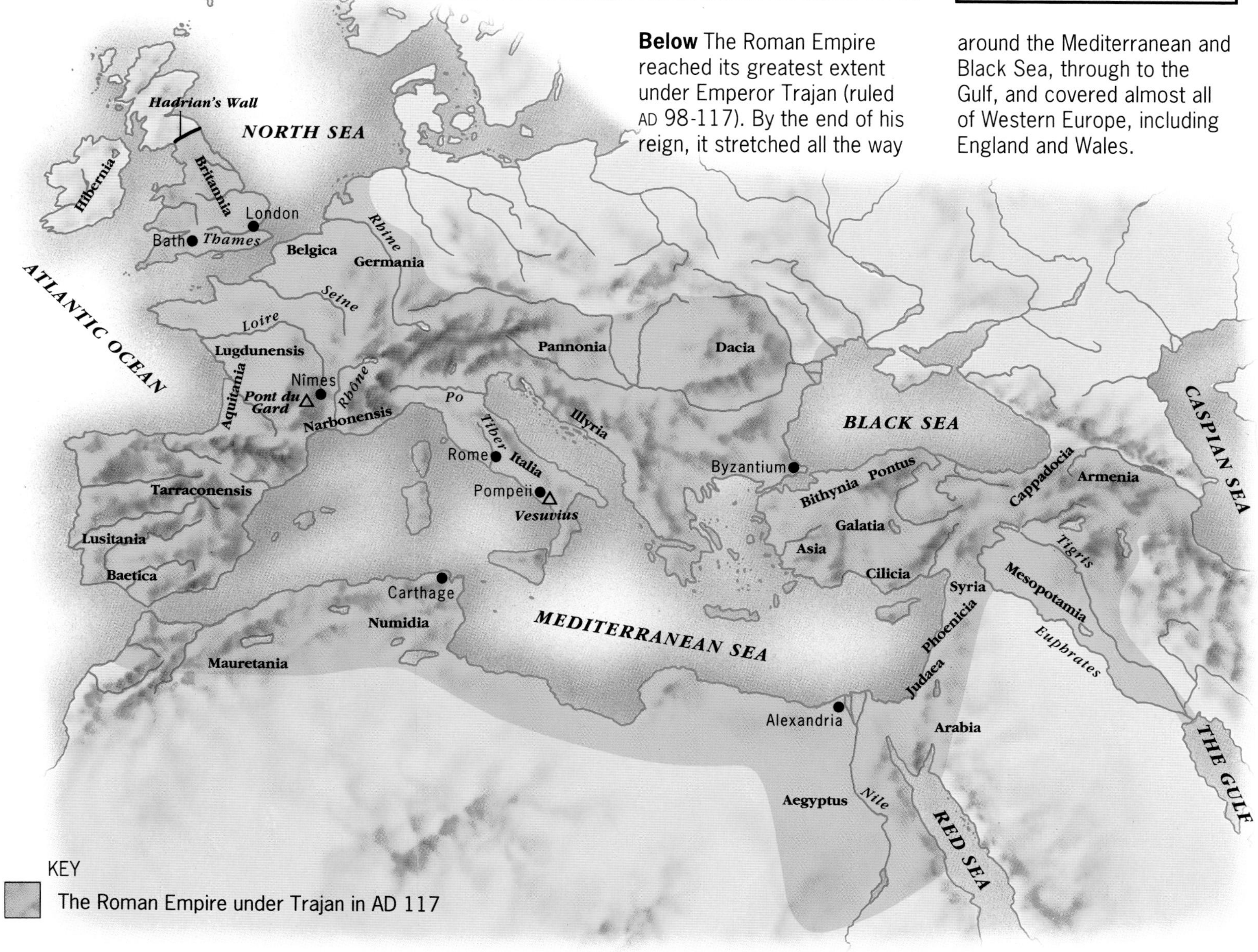

Hadrian's Wall
NORTH SEA
Hibernia
Britannia
London
Bath
Thames
Belgica
Rhine
Germania
ATLANTIC OCEAN
Seine
Loire
Lugdunensis
Aquitania
Nîmes
Pont du Gard
Rhône
Narbonensis
Pannonia
Dacia
Po
Illyria
BLACK SEA
CASPIAN SEA
Tiber
Rome
Italia
Byzantium
Pontus
Bithynia
Cappadocia
Armenia
Tarraconensis
Pompeii
Vesuvius
Galatia
Lusitania
Asia
Tigris
Baetica
Cilicia
Carthage
Syria
Mesopotamia
Numidia
Phoenicia
MEDITERRANEAN SEA
Euphrates
Mauretania
Judaea
Alexandria
Arabia
THE GULF
Aegyptus
Nile
RED SEA

KEY

The Roman Empire under Trajan in AD 117

THE CELTS

In the centuries when the Romans were still confined to Italy, central and northern Europe were dominated by a group of people known as the Celts.

The Celts originated in the region of Switzerland and southwestern Germany and the key to their success was iron-working. After 400 BC they spread rapidly throughout most of Europe, taking advantage of their iron weapons. One group of Celts, called Gauls by the Romans, sacked Rome in 390 BC. Others invaded Greece and sacked Delphi in 279 BC, then went on to settle in Turkey where they became known as the Galatians.

The Celts used chariots and were famous for their fighting skills on horseback. Celtic horsemen wore trousers—the first in Europe. They were ruled by chiefs and lived in fortified villages, in thatched houses with walls of rough stone or of wattle and daub (interwoven branches covered with mud).

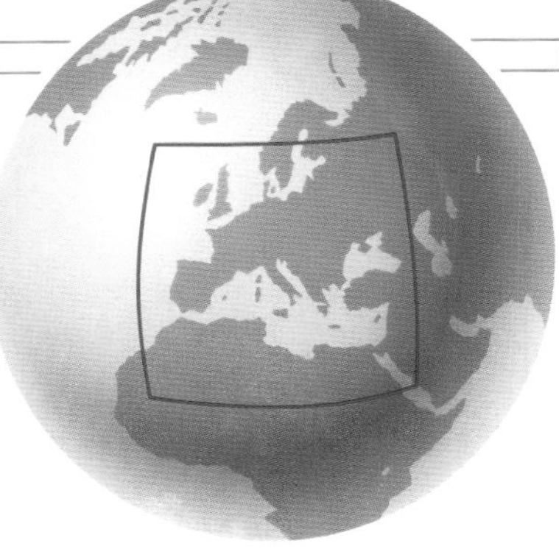

Left Many of the Celts adopted Christianity after the 5th century AD. They applied the intricate pattern of Celtic design to their stone crosses.

Their religious leaders were the powerful Druids. Although the Romans, their long-time enemies, portrayed the Celts as wild and barbaric, the beautifully crafted Celtic metalwork indicates more sophisticated ways of life.

The Romans eventually conquered the Celts in western Europe in the 1st centuries BC and AD, and the Celts were absorbed into the Roman Empire. However, Celtic culture and languages survived on the fringes of the empire—in Brittany, Cornwall, Ireland, and Scotland, where the Celtic heritage is still cherished today.

Repelling attackers

Typical sites for Celtic settlements were hilltops and islands on lakes, both of which provide natural defenses against enemies. Hill forts, such as Maiden Castle (above) near Dorchester in southern England, were fortified by rings of earthworks (embankments), which were so massive that they can still be seen today, even after 2,000 years of weathering. High wooden palisades lined the crests of the earthworks. Inside the protection of the fortifications there were houses, pits for storing grain, and pens for farm animals.

Occupied since Neolithic times, Maiden Castle was developed by the Celts around 300 BC. In the 1st century BC the fortifications had to be extended because the range of slingshot, the new weapon, was over 100 yards (90 m). The fort was eventually conquered by the Romans in AD 44.

Pagan traditions

The Druids provided a vital link between the Celts and their gods. They made sure that the correct rituals were carried out. They were also teachers and the guardians of Celtic law. This engraving (above) includes the moon and oak leaves - both important elements in Druid rituals. There were four great festivals each year. The Feast of Samhain on October 31 has survived as Halloween.

Below The Battersea Shield, found in the Thames River in London, shows the typical swirling pattern of Celtic design. Made of bronze, it was probably used for ceremonial occasions rather than for warfare.

Masters of iron

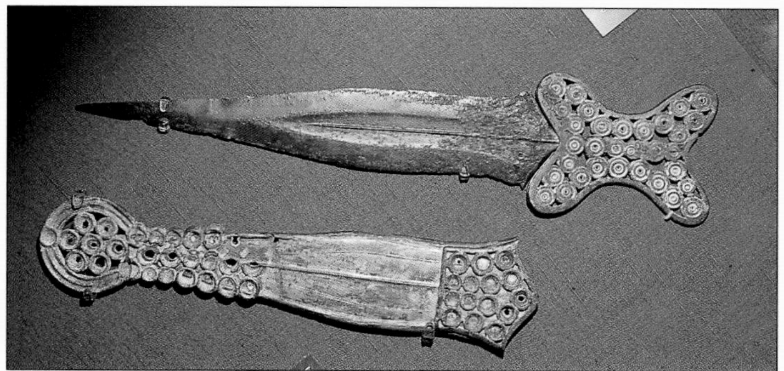

The secret of iron-working reached central Europe by about the 7th century BC. Hallstatt, in Austria, became the main center. Like other early iron-smelters before them, the Celts found that whoever possessed iron technology had an immediate advantage over their Bronze Age neighbors. Iron weapons were stronger and more durable, and iron could also be made into more efficient tools, such as axes for clearing forests and plows for tilling the land.

The Celts applied their skills as craftsmen to their weapons. The blades were made of iron, but the handles and sheaths were often made of bronze, which was more easily worked and so could be decorated with Celtic patterning. Jewelry—notably the heavy neck rings called torques worn by the warriors—was also made of bronze as well as of silver and gold.

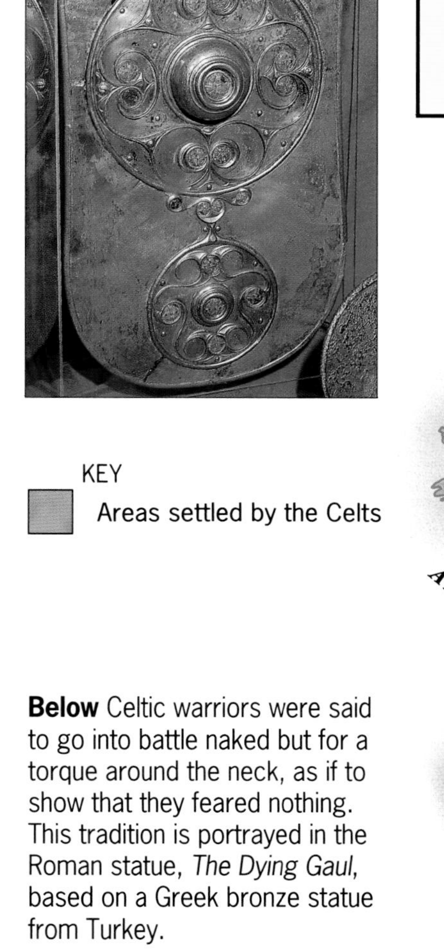

KEY

Areas settled by the Celts

SCOTLAND

NORTH SEA

IRELAND

BRITAIN

London

Thames

Maiden Castle

Cornwall

Rhine

ATLANTIC OCEAN

Seine

Brittany

Loire

GAUL

Danube

La Tène

Hallstatt

Rhône

Po

Tiber

Rome

BLACK SEA

SPAIN

GREECE

Galatia

Delphi

TURKEY

MEDITERRANEAN SEA

Below Celtic warriors were said to go into battle naked but for a torque around the neck, as if to show that they feared nothing. This tradition is portrayed in the Roman statue, *The Dying Gaul*, based on a Greek bronze statue from Turkey.

Above By about 200 BC the Celts had spread throughout most of northern and central Europe, and east as far as the Black Sea. There were also Celts in Spain and in western Turkey. After the 1st century AD only the Celts in Ireland and Scotland remained beyond the reach of the Roman Empire.

THE BARBARIANS

The word "barbarian" was originally used by the Greeks to refer to people who were not Greek. Later it was used by the Romans for people from outside the borders of their empire.

The Barbarian invasion of the Roman Empire began when the Huns of Central Asia began forcing the Germanic tribes from north and east of the Rhine and Danube rivers westward around AD 375. The Visigoths (West Goths) were pushed into Roman territory, but were treated harshly. They rebelled and defeated the Romans, and, under Alaric, sacked Rome in AD 410. In AD 406 the Vandals and Sueves attacked Gaul, and then were pushed on by the Visigoths. The Sueves set up a kingdom in Galicia, and the Vandals moved on to North Africa.

With their homelands increasingly under threat, the Romans withdrew from Britain in AD 407, leaving the country open to attack by the Angles and Saxons, another group of Germanic tribes. The Huns under Attila (reigned AD 433-453) attacked Gaul in AD 451, but were defeated by the Romans and their new allies, the Visigoths. Attila now turned on Italy, but spared Rome. The Ostrogoths (East Goths) then occupied Italy, while the Franks (see pages 54-55) occupied northern France.

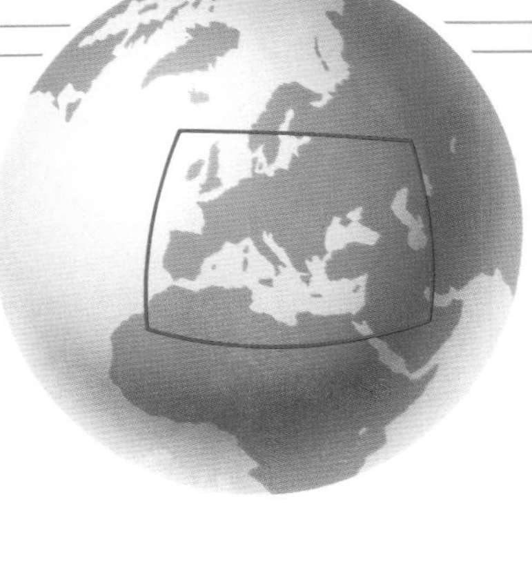

Left King Reccesvinth's crown, made about AD 650, forms part of the Treasures of Gurrazar that were found in Toledo, the Visigothic capital of Spain. Made of gold and richly encrusted in jewels, it was designed to hang over a Christian altar. Because of the uncertainties of this period, the treasures of the "wandering nations" tended to be objects that could be packed away quickly, to be hidden or carried to safety.

The Ostrogoths and the Vandals were later defeated by the Byzantine Emperor Justinian in the 6th century (see pages 52-53), and the Visigoths were conquered in Spain by the Moors in the 8th century (see pages 32-33).

Below Despite their superior weapons, discipline, and training, the Romans both feared and respected Barbarian warriors for their determination and their unconventional battle tactics. They also employed them to assist their own troops as mercenaries. This panel is from the Arch of Constantine, erected in Rome in AD 315.

Above This gold and enamel brooch demonstrates the great skills and craftsmanship of Anglo-Saxons. The richness of Anglo-Saxon life in England was brought vividly to light by the discovery of the Sutton Hoo ship burial in Suffolk, dating from about AD 635. The treasure also included jewelry, armor, and weapons from the Roman, Frankish, and Byzantine empires.

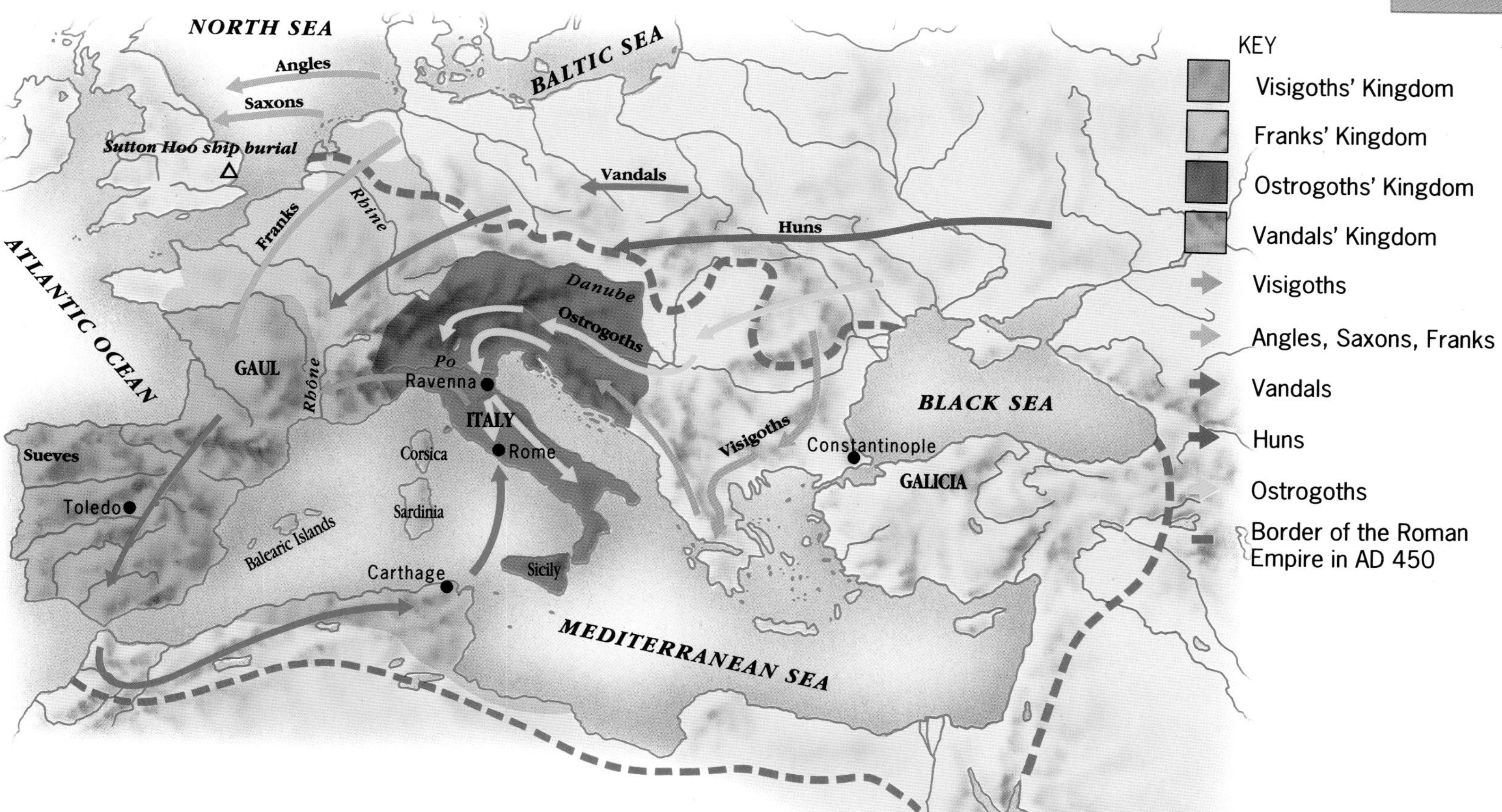

NORTH SEA
BALTIC SEA
ATLANTIC OCEAN
BLACK SEA
MEDITERRANEAN SEA
Angles
Saxons
Sutton Hoo ship burial
Franks
Rhine
Vandals
Huns
Danube
Ostrogoths
Po
Ravenna
GAUL
Rhône
ITALY
Rome
Corsica
Sardinia
Balearic Islands
Sicily
Carthage
Sueves
Toledo
Visigoths
Constantinople
GALICIA

KEY
Visigoths' Kingdom
Franks' Kingdom
Ostrogoths' Kingdom
Vandals' Kingdom
Visigoths
Angles, Saxons, Franks
Vandals
Huns
Ostrogoths
Border of the Roman Empire in AD 450

Above Following their turbulent movements across the Roman Empire from Central Europe and Asia in the 4th and 5th centuries AD, the Barbarians settled into four main kingdoms: the Ostrogoths, the Franks, the Visigoths, and the Vandals. Only the Franks survived the rise of the Byzantine and Islamic empires.

Vandalism

The Vandals earned their reputation, and their place in the English language as wreckers and spoilers, by sacking Rome in AD 455. The Vandals were a Germanic race that had first occupied Spain, but were challenged there by the Visigoths. In AD 429, led by King Gaiseric, they crossed over to North Africa and conquered the old Roman provinces around Carthage. They built up an impressive fleet, and then captured the Balearic Islands, Corsica, Sardinia, and part of Sicily. Despite their reputation for plunder, they were also settlers, and mainly Christian. This mosaic from Carthage dates from the Vandal era. The Vandals' territories were retaken in the 530s by the Byzantine army under general Belisarius.

Above Ravenna, in north-eastern Italy, became the capital of the Ostrogoth Empire under King Odoacer (reigned AD 476-493). Sent by the Byzantine Empire, Theodoric the Great defeated Odoacer, then killed him to take the Ostrogoth crown for himself (reigned 493-526).

As in other Barbarian kingdoms, the Ostrogoths saw themselves to some extent as the heirs to Roman civilization. This grand, circular mausoleum built around AD 520 to house Theodoric's tomb, shows the influence of Roman architecture.

It is still a mystery how the builders installed the huge dome, which is made from a single piece of limestone weighing 300 tons.

THE BYZANTINE EMPIRE

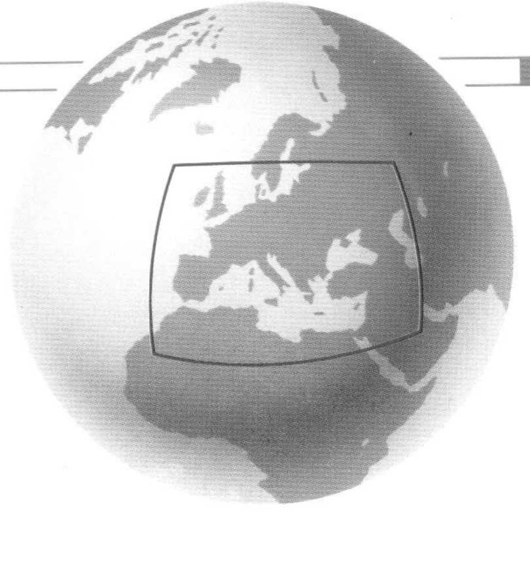

The Roman Empire (see pages 46-47) was divided in two in AD 395. The center of the Eastern Roman Empire was the old Greek city of Byzantium, rebuilt as a capital city by Emperor Constantine I (reigned AD 310-337) and renamed Constantinople.

The Byzantines saw themselves as Romans, and jealously preserved many of the traditions of Roman and Greek civilization that had been erased in the West by the chaos of the Barbarian invasions (see pages 50-51). But they were also Christians, and so their empire had a new and quite distinct character.

In a remarkable series of campaigns during the 6th century, Emperor Justinian (reigned AD 527-565) won back many territories of the old Roman Empire, pushing the Vandals out of North Africa and defeating the Ostrogoths in Italy. But over the next two centuries many of these were lost.

The fortunes of the Byzantines waxed and waned over the next 500 years. A Crusader army (see pages 58-59) sacked Constantinople in 1204 and established the Latin Empire there, while what remained of the Byzantine Empire in Greece and Asia Minor split up into the separate states of Nicaea, Trebizond, and Epirus. The Byzantines drove out the Latins and reestablished their emperor in Constantinople. The Ottomans, the new power in the region, gradually closed in, and put an end to the Byzantine Empire when they captured Constantinople in 1453.

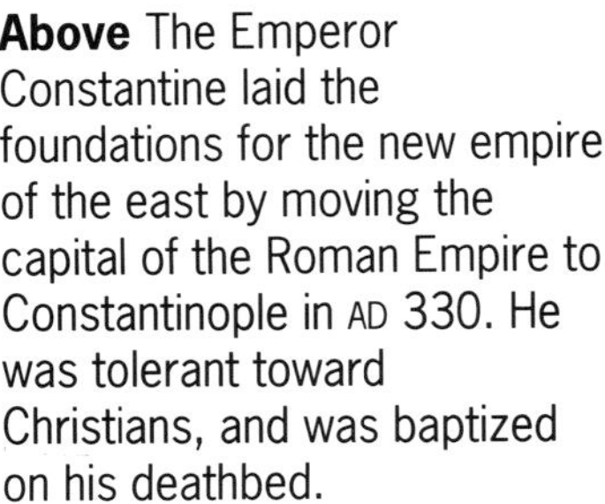

Above The Emperor Constantine laid the foundations for the new empire of the east by moving the capital of the Roman Empire to Constantinople in AD 330. He was tolerant toward Christians, and was baptized on his deathbed.

Right Byzantine craftsmen were famous for their ivory carving. This ivory from about AD 500 depicts a contest between men and bears, watched by an audience. Similar shows had been popular in ancient Rome.

Glittering portraits

Ravenna already had a tradition of exceptionally beautiful mosaics before it was conquered by Justinian in 540 and became the capital of Byzantine Italy. The churches themselves look fairly ordinary from the outside, but inside they glitter with the thousands of small tiles that cover entire walls.

A mosaic picture (left) in the Church of San Vitale in Ravenna is a portrait of Byzantine power: Justinian (with a halo indicating his semi-sacred status) stands with his courtiers, including Archbishop Maximian, who consecrated the church in AD 547. The soldiers, seen to the far left, represent the military might of the Byzantine Empire.

The Byzantines were also known for their painted portraits of Christ and the saints, called icons, which became objects of reverence. When the empire went into decline after the 7th century, some people interpreted this as a punishment by God angered by the worship of icons. These "iconoclasts" (icon-breakers) destroyed icons and, like the Muslims, forbade any attempt to portray people in religious art. The iconoclasts remained a powerful political force from AD 720 to 843.

Left The church of Hagia Sophia (Saint Sophia) was the great masterpiece of Byzantine architecture. It was built in Constantinople between AD 532 and 537 on the orders of Justinian. It became a mosque after the fall of Constantinople in 1453. The Ottomans added the minarets and Islamic inscriptions but otherwise left the building intact.

Below The fall of Constantinople to the Ottoman Empire was a major blow to Western Europe. It marked the end of Roman history, the loss of the last Christian power in the Eastern Mediterranean, and the complete domination of the Ottomans over trade through this vital region.

Below Under Justinian, the Byzantine Empire occupied most of the territories of the old Roman Empire around the Mediterranean. After the various invasions in the 7th and 8th centuries, however, its territories were restricted to Asia Minor and the coasts around the Aegean Sea.

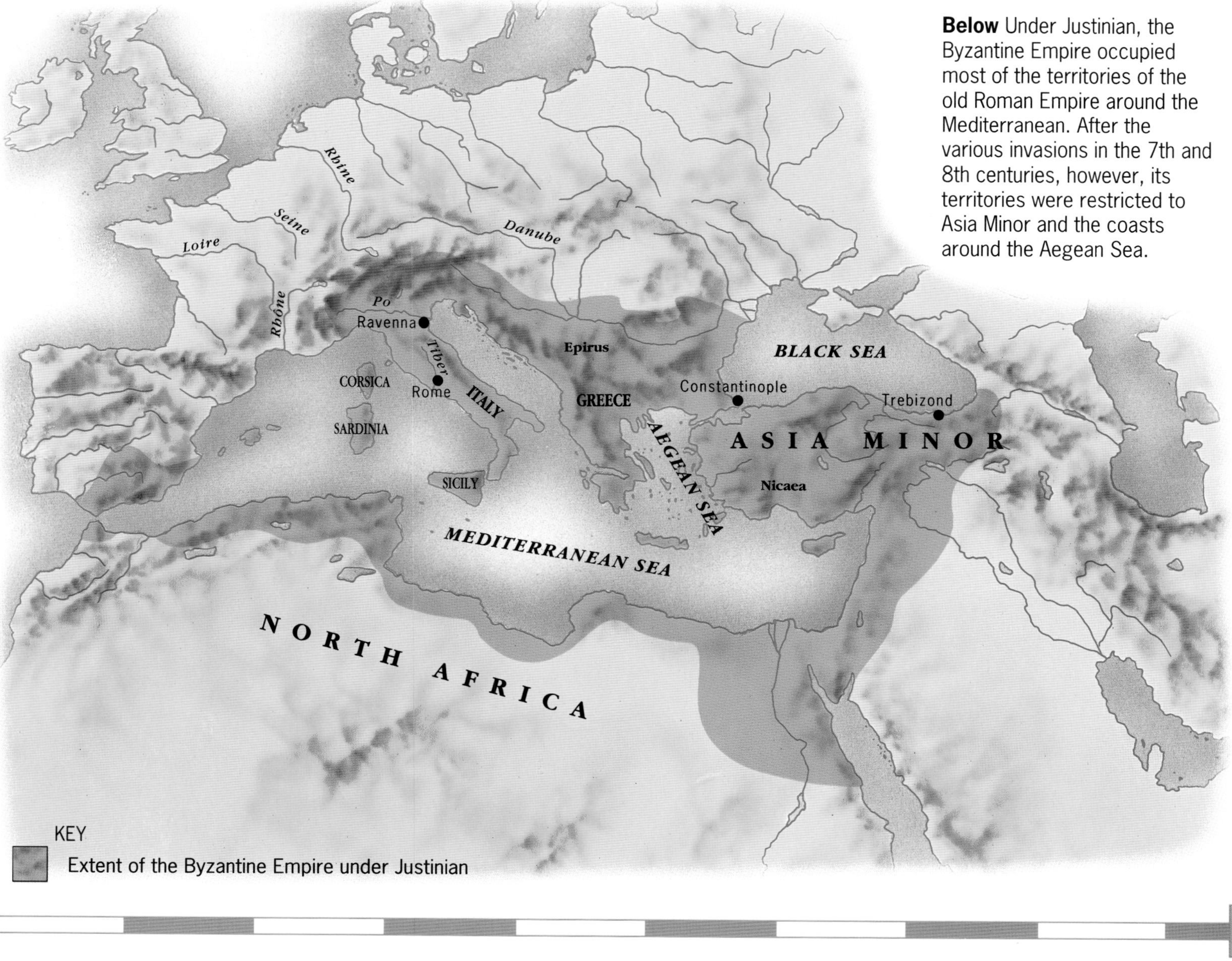

THE FRANKS

As the Roman Empire collapsed in Western Europe (see pages 50-51), various tribes swiftly filled the vacuum the departing Romans left behind. In northern Europe the most numerous were the Franks, a Germanic tribe from the Rhine region whose people had been used as mercenaries by the Romans.

Under their chief, Clovis I (reigned AD 481-511), the Franks invaded Roman Gaul in AD 486 and pushed back the Visigoths to the south of the Pyrenees. Clovis founded the Merovingian Dynasty, named after Merovech, a previous chief of the Franks, and was converted to Christianity in AD 496.

While other Barbarian kingdoms fell to the Byzantines (see pages 52-53) and the Arabs (see pages 32-33), the Franks survived and extended their territory. The Merovingian Dynasty lasted until AD 751, but over time an increasing amount of power was given to the chief court officials called the "Mayors of the Palace." One of these, Charles Martel, was celebrated for defeating the advancing Muslims in AD 732. His son, Pepin the Short, overthrew the last Merovingian king and became the first king (reigned AD 751-768) of the Carolingian Dynasty (from *Carolus*, Latin for Charles).

Pepin's son Charlemagne (reigned AD 768-814) was the greatest Frankish ruler. However, by the time of his death the empire was already under stress, and increasingly harassed by Viking raiders (see pages 56-57).

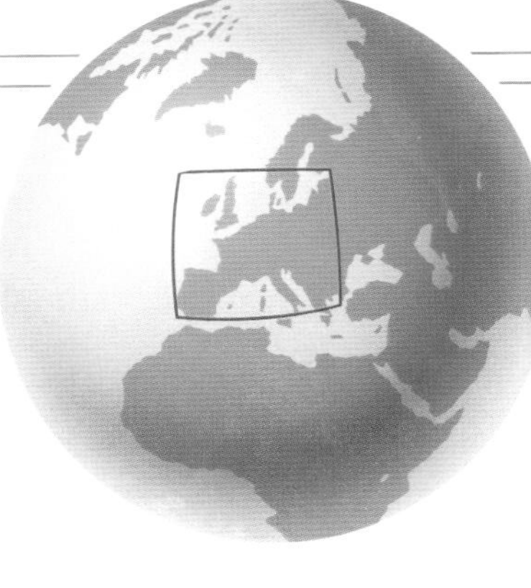

Left In the turbulent times of the early Frankish kingdoms, treasures were often small and easy to carry, such as this buckle inlaid with silver.

Charlemagne

Charles the Great, better known as Charlemagne, saw himself as the heir to the Roman Empire. He was crowned Emperor of the Romans by the Pope in Rome on Christmas Day AD 800.

This 19th-century painting gives an impression of the coronation.

Charlemagne created an efficient administration for his huge empire, and his court at Aachen became a great center for scholars and artists of all kinds.

But after Charlemagne's reign the kingdom was split up. East Francia later evolved into Germany. West Francia became France; the Franks' language, which had evolved in Gaul under the Romans, became known as French.

Above Charlemagne was much revered as a Christian king. This gold and silver bust, from Aachen Cathedral, was made in his honor in 1349.

Above The court of Charlemagne became a center for Christian scholarship, and many beautifully illustrated (or "illuminated") books were produced during his reign.

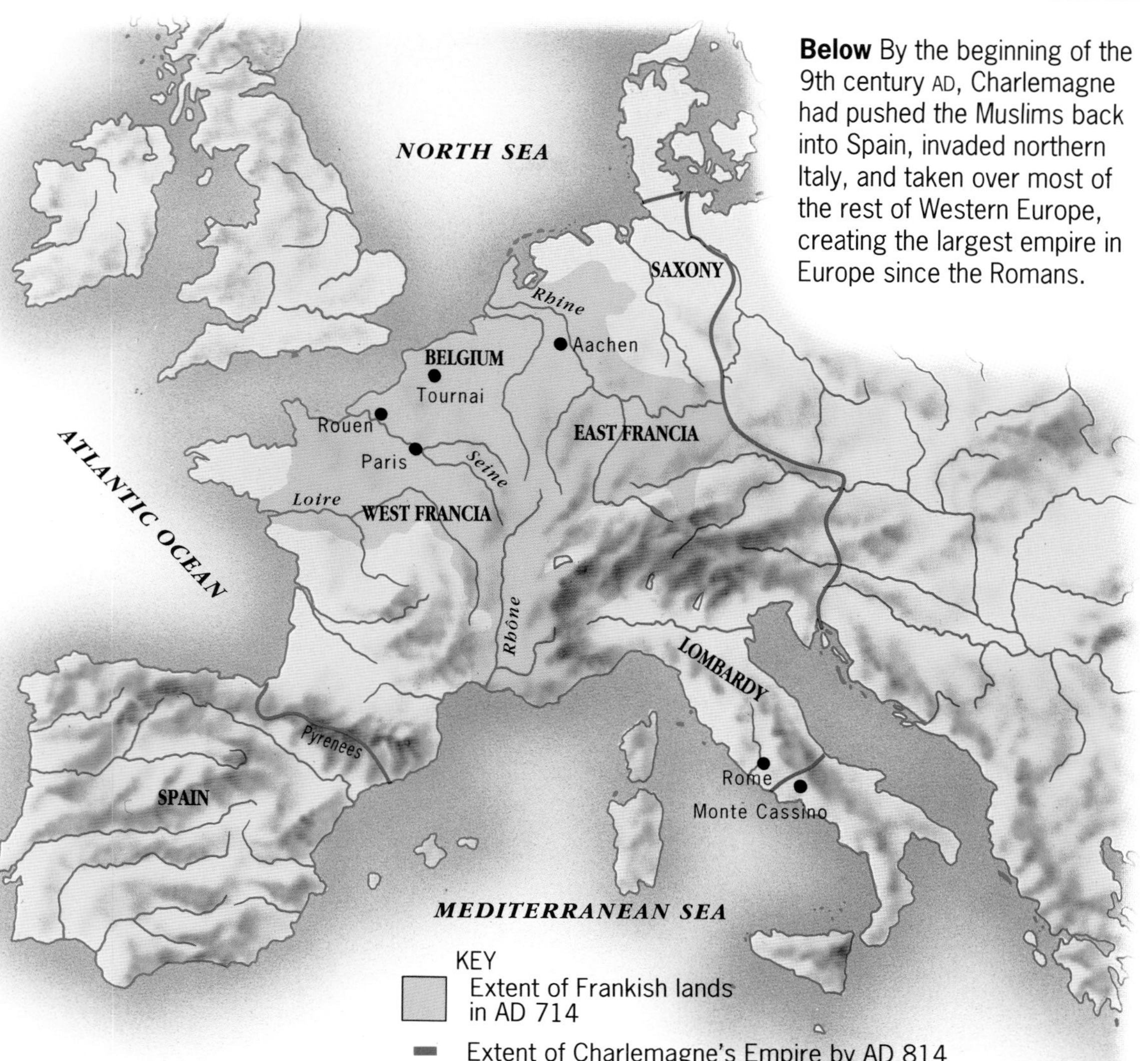

Below By the beginning of the 9th century AD, Charlemagne had pushed the Muslims back into Spain, invaded northern Italy, and taken over most of the rest of Western Europe, creating the largest empire in Europe since the Romans.

Ringing the changes

Bell towers were developed in Charlemagne's era, stamping the landscape with prominent symbols of Christianity. Bells called the faithful to prayer at regular intervals during the day, and so acted as a simple kind of clock. They were also used to sound the alarm when danger threatened.

A life of prayer

Many Christian monasteries in Europe were founded during the Frankish Empire. Christianity had a tradition of hermits, who retreated from the world to lead simple lives devoted to prayer. Monasteries pursued the same tradition, but brought together large numbers of monks in single organizations. St. Benedict (about 480-547) founded the first European monastic order, the Benedictines, who gradually spread out from their first monastery at Monte Cassino in Italy. Other monastic orders, such as the Cistercians, Dominicans, and Franciscans, were founded later. Monasteries like this one at Cluny, near Lyons in France, became the most important centers for learning in Europe until the Renaissance (see pages 60-61). Some also became extremely rich.

THE VIKINGS

The Vikings (or Norsemen) were warriors from Scandinavia who terrorized Europe from the late 8th to 11th centuries. They raided towns and monasteries for treasure and supplies of food, and enslaved their victims. The Vikings were skilled in shipbuilding; their sleek ships could withstand the ocean and also travel far inland by river. They inspired great terror: the word berserk derives from a wild Viking warrior called a *berserkr* (meaning "bear-shirt") who dressed and fought like an enraged beast. The greatest honor for a warrior was to die in battle and then enjoy fighting and feasting in the palace of Valhalla, the mythical Viking world of dead heroes.

But this is not the whole story. The Vikings were also traders and settlers. Vikings from Sweden traveled across eastern Europe and traded with merchants from the Middle East. Known as Varangians or Rus, Swedish Vikings established powerful Russian states, including one based on Kiev.

Vikings from Denmark and Norway settled in Britain, Germany, Ireland, France, and Spain in the very places they raided. They were intrepid travelers and also went as far as Iceland and Greenland. In about AD 1000, Vikings from the Greenland settlement, sailing under the leadership of Leif Eriksson, probably reached North America.

Above The Vikings were gifted craftsmen who embellished their ships, weapons, and tools with carvings. This head comes from a cart found in the 9th-century ship burial of Oseberg, Norway. Like much of Viking carving, it transmits a sense of vigorous energy.

Below The culture of the Vikings was centered on their ships. Great nobles were buried—or cremated—in them, along with weapons, household objects, food, and even slain horses, dogs, and slaves. Ordinary people might be buried in a small boat, or at least in a grave marked with stones in the shape of a boat. Burial sites have become one of the main sources of our knowledge about the Vikings.

Viking gods

The main god of the Vikings was Odin (or Wodan), ruler of Valhalla. His son Thor was a sky god, and god of law and order, who would throw his hammer at unruly monsters. Small images of his hammer (below) were worn as a protection against evil. Tiu was a god of war. Freya was a fertility goddess. These gods are still with us: Tuesday is Tiu's day, Wednesday is Wodan's day, Thursday is Thor's day, and Friday is Freya's day.

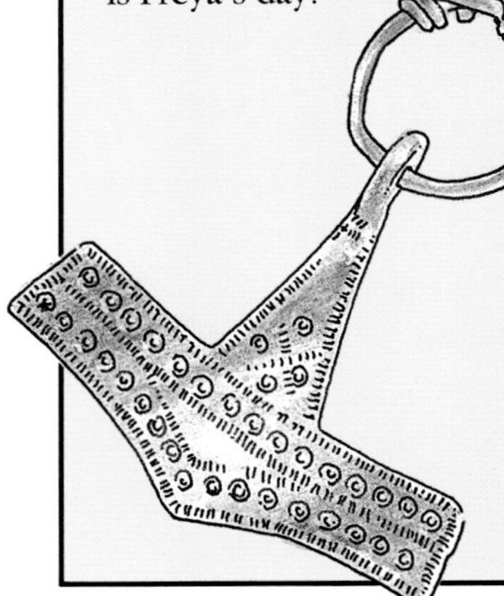

Masters of the sea

The ships that have survived almost intact in burial sites show clearly the Vikings' great mastery of shipbuilding. Their war vessels, or longships, were up to 92 feet (28 m) in length, and powered by the wind in their square sails and sixteen or so pairs of oars. They carried crews of about 60 men, who acted as both sailors and warriors. Their trading vessels were heavier, broader, and slower ships called *knorrs*.

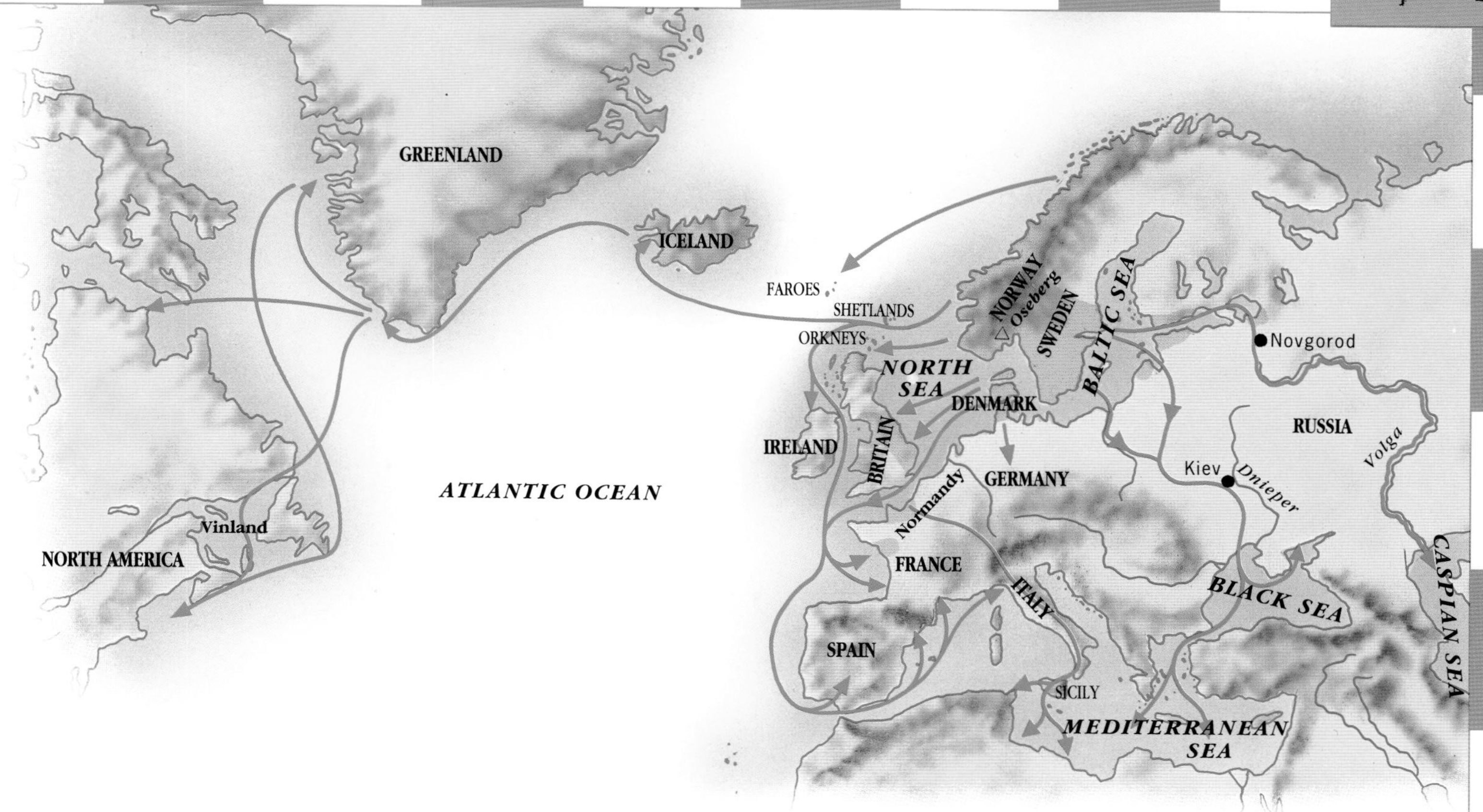

Above The Vikings came from numerous communities in Norway, Sweden, and Denmark, many of which were situated in harsh and remote landscapes. Their background partly explains why the wealthy, fertile coasts of Europe proved such tempting places for the Vikings to raid and to found settlements. It also suggests why they were able to adapt to the difficult conditions of Iceland and Greenland.

KEY

 Lands from which the Vikings came

 Viking settlements

Viking routes

Arab connection

Swedish Vikings traded and plundered extensively throughout eastern Europe. They traveled down the Dnieper River to the Black Sea, and down the Volga River to the Caspian Sea, where they encountered traders from the Byzantine Empire (see pages 52-53) and Islamic Empire (see pages 32-33). They exchanged slaves and furs for silks and spices.

Norman conquests

Norse raiders regularly plundered the River Seine as far as Paris. To appease them, the French King, Charles the Simple (reigned AD 879-931) granted them a region of northern France, which became known as Normandy. The power of the Dukes of Normandy grew. They conquered not only England in 1066, but also southern Italy and Sicily.

Below Compared to the rest of Europe, the Vikings were slow to adopt Christianity. However, the Normans became Christian during the 10th century, and Christianity gradually replaced the religion of Odin and Thor in Scandinavia during the next century. The remarkable "stave churches" in Norway are among the oldest wooden buildings in the world. This one, at Borgund, dates from 1150.

FEUDAL EUROPE

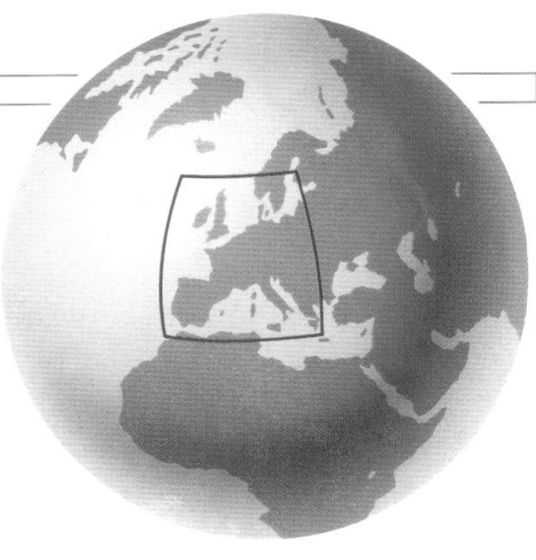

The chaotic and violent times in Europe during the 9th and 10th centuries demanded a system of government that could provide protection for the community. The feudal system was the answer, and for most people the cost of this protection was their freedom.

In the feudal system, the king owned all the land, but granted it to nobles and knights in return for their support. They rented their land to various lords of the manor, who in turn parceled it out to tenants, the poorest of whom (the serfs and villeins) were also obliged to work the lord's land. They paid the lord of the manor with a percentage of their crops, and also fought for him if asked to do so. On some estates, or domains, the serfs existed in a state of near-slavery; in others they were comparatively free. Under this system kings and nobles could call upon armies of loyal supporters, as well as large pools of labor to build their castles.

Feudalism was practiced in France, Spain, Italy, and Germany for much of the medieval period. The Normans brought it to England after 1066. The system began to change with new methods of warfare, the growth of trade and towns, and the rise of a middle class of merchants, traders, and shopkeepers. When the Black Death struck in the mid 14th century, it devastated Europe's populations and caused such a shortage of labor that feudalism could no longer function properly. The renting of land became more flexible, and more people were now paid wages for work, giving greater freedom to the vast majority.

Below The economy of Europe during the feudal period was based on agriculture. This illumination from a 14th-century book of sacred songs shows two farmers working the fields. Life was hard for the laborers, who worked long hours from an early age.

Safety in an uncertain world

Josselin Castle in Brittany, France, built in the 11th and 14th centuries, is typical of the mighty fortresses of the great feudal lords. Those castles were designed to withstand attack and siege, but they were also impressive palaces where the lord could live grandly with his large household and provide lavish entertainment for his guests.

Above Under the feudal system the church became extremely wealthy. By far the most impressive buildings in medieval cities, cathedrals were designed to leave the beholder in no doubt about the glory of God, and the power and splendor of his Church. The cathedral of Chartres, in northern France, was built during the 12th and 13th centuries. It is particularly famous for its beautiful stained-glass windows, many of which still contain the original glass installed in 1150. They fill most of the walls, lighting up the interior like a huge magic lantern.

Left The Christian kingdoms of Europe saw the rise of Islam (see pages 32-33) as a direct threat to their trading and religious interests. Between the 11th and 13th centuries they launched a series of Crusades against the Islamic Empire. These were very costly and only temporarily successful.

Above Much of the finest artistic work of the feudal period was done for the Church, which could afford to employ the best artists and craftsmen. On the 12th-century Troyes Casket, gilded and enameled pictures illustrate the triumph of the virtues over the vices.

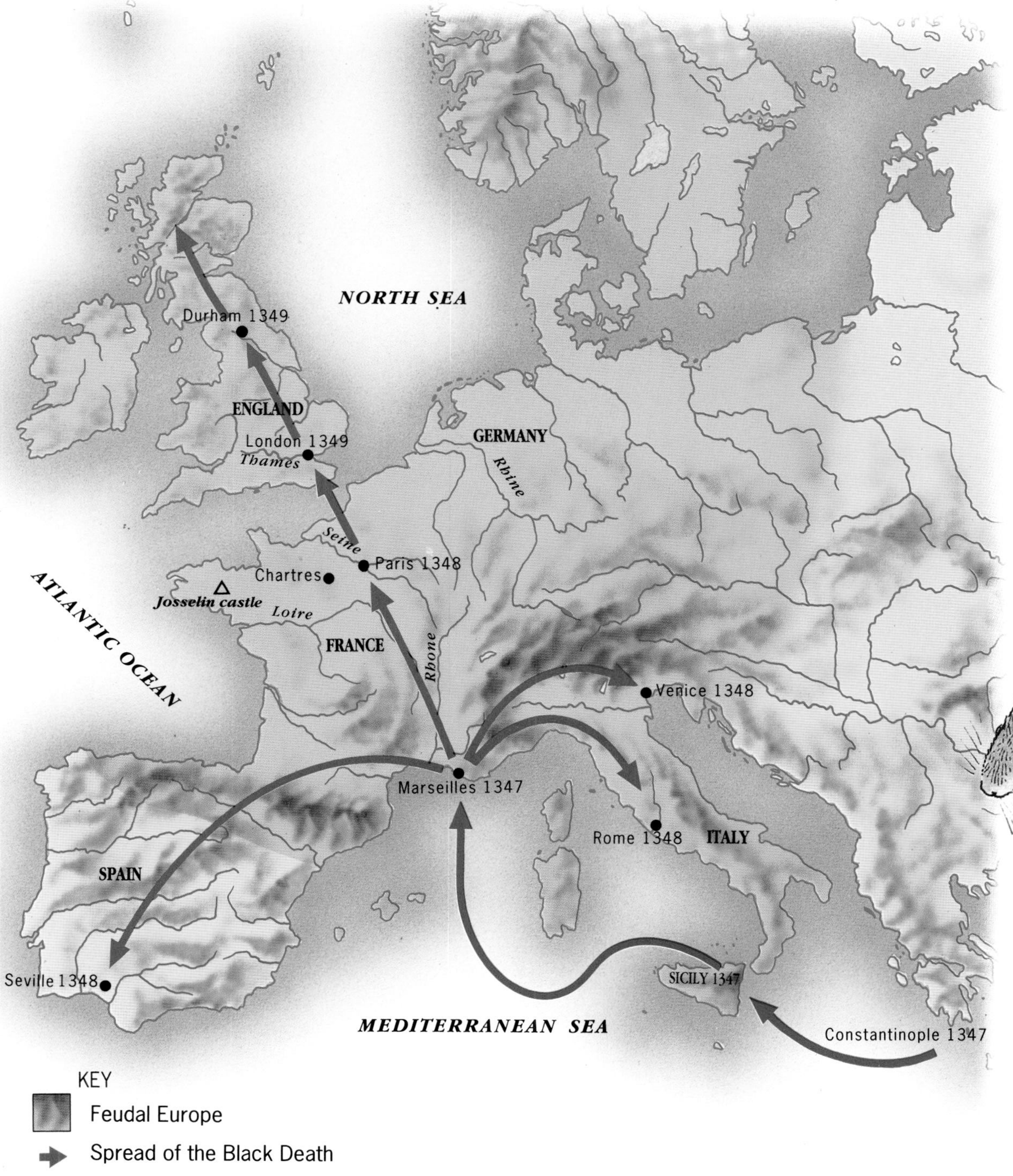

NORTH SEA
Durham 1349
ENGLAND
London 1349
Thames
GERMANY
Rhine
Seine
Paris 1348
Chartres
Josselin castle
Loire
FRANCE
ATLANTIC OCEAN
Rhone
Venice 1348
Marseilles 1347
Rome 1348
ITALY
SPAIN
Seville 1348
SICILY 1347
MEDITERRANEAN SEA
Constantinople 1347

KEY
Feudal Europe
Spread of the Black Death

The Black Death

Bubonic plague, called the Black Death, started in the Far East and was brought to Europe on merchant ships. It was transmitted by fleas carried on rats. Victims suffered from fever and developed black lumps or "buboes" on their skin. There was no known cure in medieval times, and the death rate was very high. It has been estimated that more than a quarter of the population of Europe died from the Black Death between 1348 and 1349.

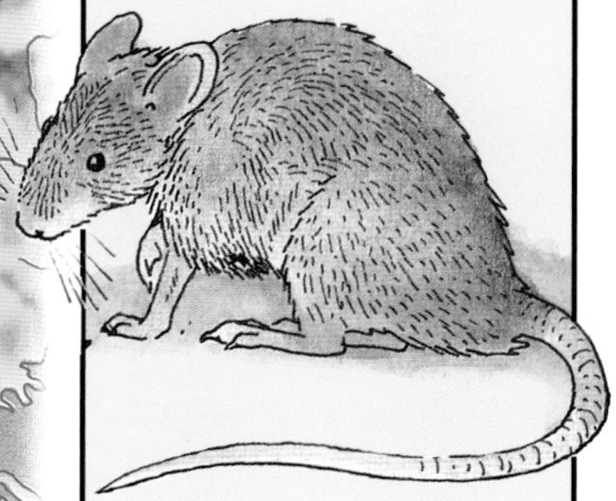

Left France, Spain, Italy, Germany, and England all adopted feudal systems, but these varied from country to country and from domain to domain. Feudalism also prevailed in parts of Scandinavia.

RENAISSANCE EUROPE

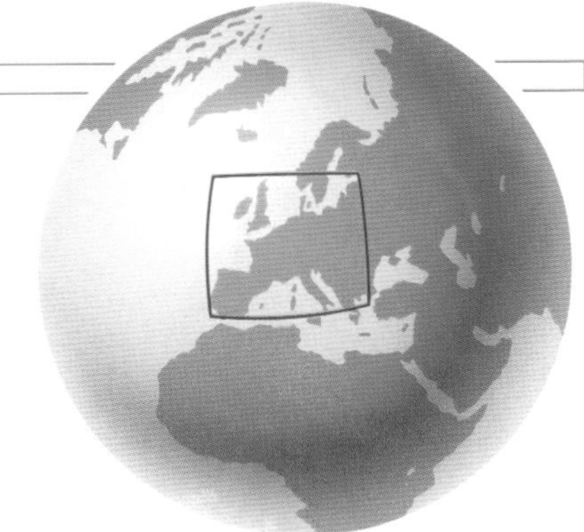

At the end of the Middle Ages there was a period when a new mood developed as scholars and artists began to ask basic questions about the world—about science, philosophy, and religion. It was called by the French word *renaissance,* which means rebirth. The scholars and artists discovered that many of their questions had been answered by the Greeks and the Romans, despite the fact that these civilizations had been pagan. It was a shock to them to find that you did not have to be Christian to be right.

This rediscovery of the classical world of the Romans and the Greeks began in Italy, where the stability and wealth of city-states such as Venice and Pisa was conducive to a revival of art and learning. Great patrons of the arts, such as the Medici family in Florence, funded new schools, universities, and libraries, and employed the greatest architects of the day to build new churches and palaces based on Roman and Greek styles.

This period coincided with the great age of European exploration. The inspiration for this was mainly the quest for trade—European merchants wanted direct access to the spices and riches of India and the Far East. But it was also part of the new quest for knowledge.

The Renaissance, which began in the 14th century, flourished in western Europe until the 17th century. In most areas—science, art, religion, government, exploration—the Renaissance provided the framework upon which modern European civilization is based.

Left The Renaissance architect Filippo Brunelleschi (1377-1446) was influenced by Roman architecture when he designed the domed cathedral of Florence.

Below Leonardo da Vinci has been described as the ultimate Renaissance man because he was an outstanding painter, scientist, and inventor. These ingenious ideas for war machines date from 1487.

Artistic freedom

During the Renaissance, the Church was still an extremely powerful patron of the arts. But artists also found new clients among wealthy merchant families. They now painted portraits, landscapes, battle scenes, and all kinds of subjects that were not religious. Sandro Botticelli (about 1444-1510), a Florentine, painted a number of famous pictures showing scenes from Roman mythology. This detail (above) from his painting called *Primavera* (Spring), depicts Flora, a Roman goddess of flowers and fertility.

In previous centuries the Church dominated both art and learning. The new freedom of artists went hand in hand with a freedom for thinkers, some of whom now began to question the Church itself.

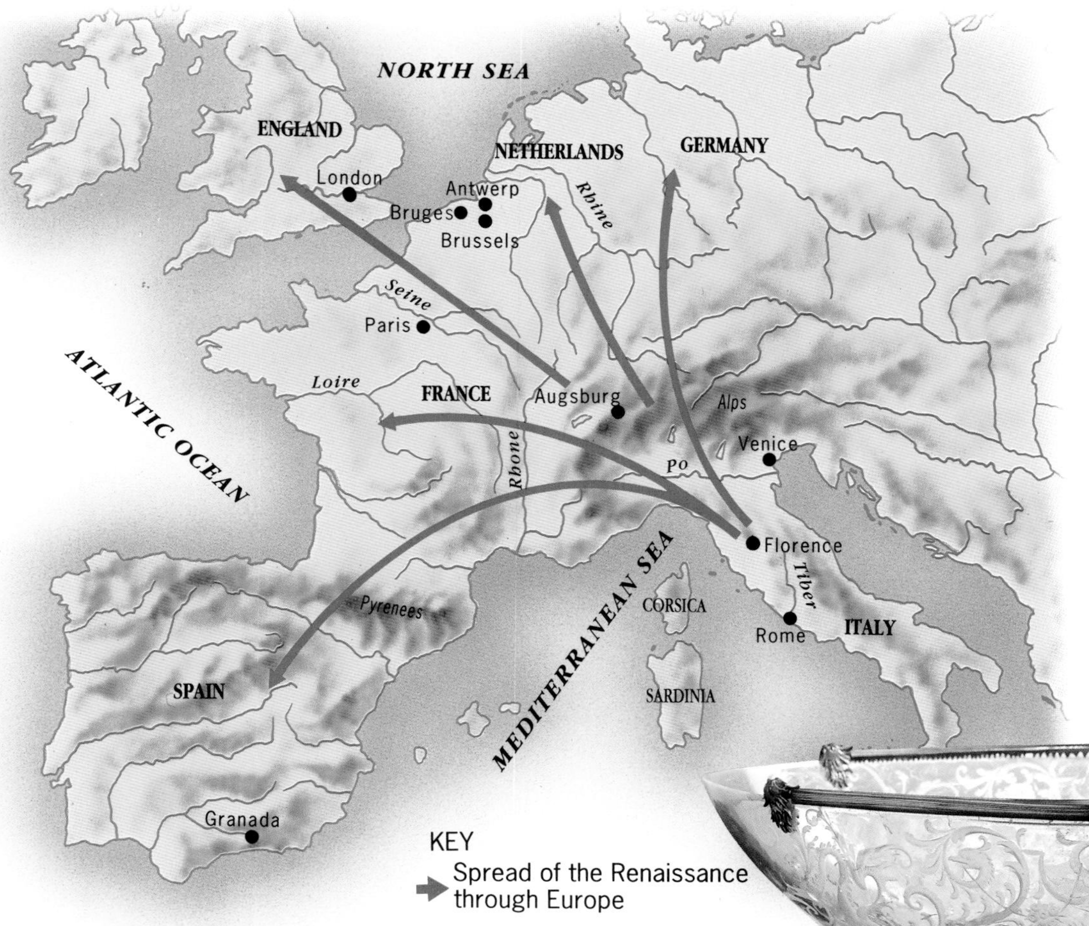

Below Wealthy Renaissance patrons encouraged craftsmen to work to very high standards. They used precious materials and produced many objects that were pure luxuries, such as this 15th-century tablepiece of rock crystal and gold.

Above The Renaissance began in Italy in the 14th century. From there it spread to France, the Netherlands, Germany, and Spain, reaching England, during the reigns of Henry VII (1485-1509) and Henry VIII (1509-1547). It affected different countries in many ways, and each put its own stamp on Renaissance ideas and artistic styles.

Above Spices and luxuries from the Far East arrived in Europe through the Middle East until the Ottoman Empire (see pages 34-35) obstructed this trade. Then Europeans set out to discover the Far East for themselves. When Christopher Columbus first landed in the Caribbean in 1492 he thought he had reached India, and the islands have been known as the West Indies ever since.

The printed word

One of the most important factors in the spread of learning and Renaissance ideas was the development of printing. A German named Johann Gutenberg (about 1397-1468) is thought to have been the first European printer to use movable type, in about 1430, although the Chinese had been using it for several centuries (see pages 72-73). Movable type makes printing much more efficient. Pages of text could now be made up quickly using a bank of individual letters.

Before printing, all books had to be written out by hand. This was very slow, and only one copy could be made at a time. Most books were made by monks and kept by the Church. Printing not only made books cheaper and quicker to produce, it also made many copies possible. This meant that the Church no longer had complete control over learning, which was now shared by the new universities, and by anyone else who was wealthy enough to buy books. Soon printing presses had sprung up all over Europe.

SECTION 6: SOUTH ASIA

Two of the world's great religions—Hinduism and Buddhism—began in South Asia and formed the basis of distinct civilizations. Islam, although it began elsewhere, was the religion of the Moguls, who later provided a spectacular flourish to South Asian culture.

Left In the Hindu religion, Kali is the goddess of destruction, and is associated with the god Shiva. She wears skulls of severed heads around her neck, and dismembered hands dangle from her belt. Terrifying though Kali is, Hindus believe that destruction is also part of rebirth and new life.

Below Christian churches are spacious buildings where the faithful gather for services. In contrast, Hindu temples in India often have little interior space and consist of richly-decorated monuments in the open air—such as this temple at Tiruchchirapalli, in southern India.

THE ARYANS

The Aryans are thought to have come from eastern Europe or southern Russia. They migrated to Iran before moving into the Indus Valley about 1500 BC (see pages 16-17). Then gradually they spread across northern India, farming and herding around the fertile banks of the Ganges River. With them they took their religion, which developed into Hinduism, as well as works of sacred literature called the *Vedas*. A central feature of their religion was caste—the division of society into rigid categories called *varnas*, fixed at birth. Following the life of Siddhartha Gautama (about 563-483 BC), known as the Buddha or "Enlightened One," Buddhism also became a major force.

Alexander the Great's army occupied the Indus Valley briefly from 326 to 325 BC (see pages 42-43). On its departure a local leader named Chandragupta Maurya rose to power, and the Mauryan Dynasty created an empire. Under King Ashoka (reigned about 270-232 BC) the Mauryans took control of most of northern India. About 263 BC, however, Ashoka took up Buddhism and renounced war, greatly influencing the spread of Buddhism in India as well as abroad.

The Mauryan Dynasty was replaced by the Hindu Sunga Dynasty about 183 BC, after which the empire split up into numerous kingdoms. These faced a period of turmoil and invasion from many peoples, including the Kushans in the 1st century AD (see pages 64-65).

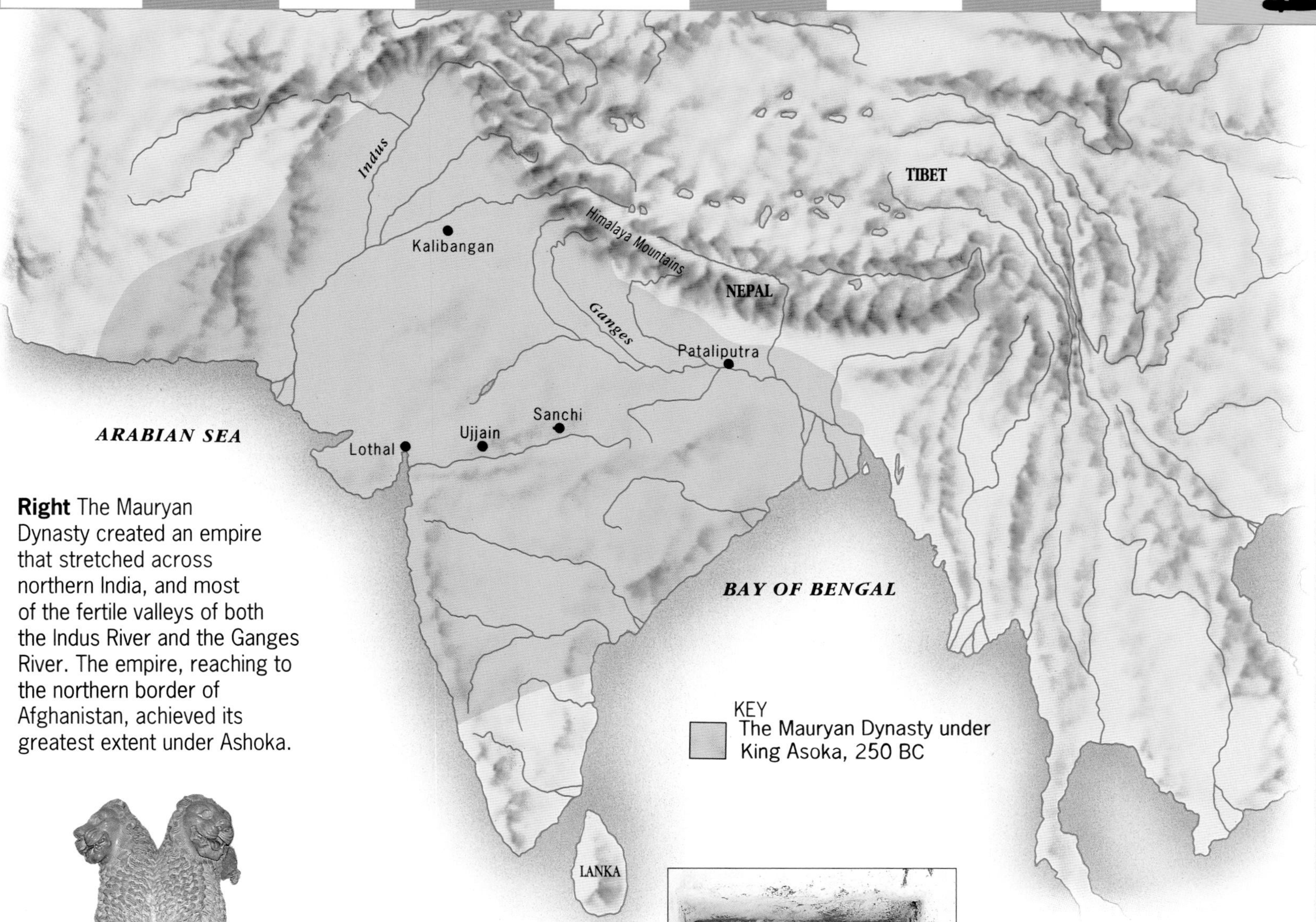

Indus
Kalibangan
Himalaya Mountains
TIBET
NEPAL
Ganges
Pataliputra
ARABIAN SEA
Lothal
Ujjain
Sanchi
BAY OF BENGAL
LANKA

KEY
The Mauryan Dynasty under King Asoka, 250 BC

Right The Mauryan Dynasty created an empire that stretched across northern India, and most of the fertile valleys of both the Indus River and the Ganges River. The empire, reaching to the northern border of Afghanistan, achieved its greatest extent under Ashoka.

Emblem of India

After victoriously waging a series of battles, Ashoka decided to turn his back on war, and developed a theory of government based on Buddhist principles. Rulers were now responsible for the welfare of their people, and had to behave correctly, with tolerance, respect, honesty, and compassion. Ashoka published his theory by having it inscribed on stone columns. On the top of the columns were four carved lions, which are now the emblem of modern India.

Right Buddhism sets out a way in which people can understand the world and be at peace with themselves through meditation and correct behavior. Statues of the Buddha are designed to show the inner calm achieved through meditation; they are not idols to be worshiped.

Below Buddhism spread throughout most of India, and was often practiced side by side with Hinduism. It also reached the remote kingdoms of the Himalayas. Here prayer wheels are turned by passers-by in the belief that, as they turn, the wheels recite sacred Buddhist chants.

THE KUSHANS AND THE GUPTAS

After the reign of Ashoka (see pages 62-63), Greek influence expanded into northern India across the border from Bactria—a breakaway state of the Seleucid Empire (see pages 42-43). This influence, spread by trade and by invasion, ended in the 1st century BC, when Scythian nomads from Central Asia, the Sakas, in turn invaded northern India.

Then in the 1st century AD the chief of another Central Asian nomadic tribe, the Kushans, united his people, invaded India, and occupied the Indus Valley and the Punjab. Under their great King Kaniska (probably 1st century AD) the Mahayana form of Buddhism spread to China along the Silk Roads, which the Kushans now controlled. The Kushans became wealthy through trade, but were frequently disrupted by invasions of northern tribes.

About AD 320 another Chandragupta (see pages 62-63), a ruler of one of the many small kingdoms of the Ganges region, created a new empire which stretched along the length of the Ganges. His son Samudra Gupta (reigned about AD 335-376) extended the empire to include the Indus Valley.

At its height, the Gupta Empire was one of the most powerful and highly developed of its time. It was noted in particular for its poetry and sculpture.

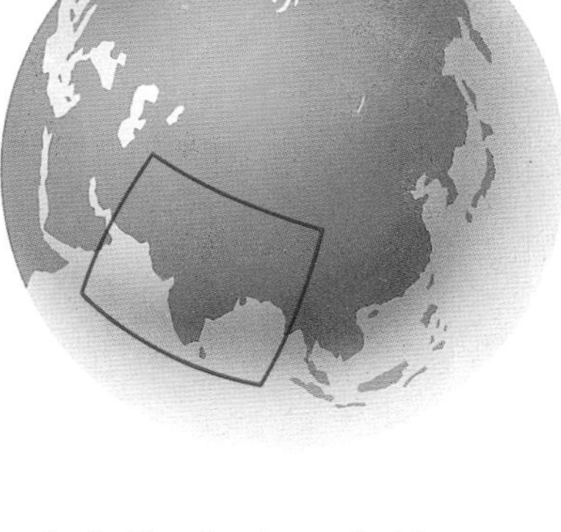

Left The Gupta period is famous for its religious carvings. Buddha figures such as this one, dating from the 5th century AD, convey a sense of the profound calm and serenity of meditation.

The Gupta Empire came to a close at the end of the 5th century AD following more invasions by people from Central Asia, this time the White Huns. After AD 700, parts of northern India were taken over by Muslim rulers and later by the Mogul Empire (see pages 68-69).

Above The Ganges River was at the heart of the Gupta Empire. It is the holiest river of the Hindus, and Varanasi (or Benares) is their most sacred city. Hindus come to bathe from the river banks, called ghats. Buddha is also known to have preached in this ancient city.

Left The Ajanta Caves are a series of about 30 caves in northern Maharashtra that evolved as dwellings and places of worship for Buddhist monks. During the time of Kumara Gupta I (reigned about AD 414-454) they were decorated with some of the best early Indian painting.

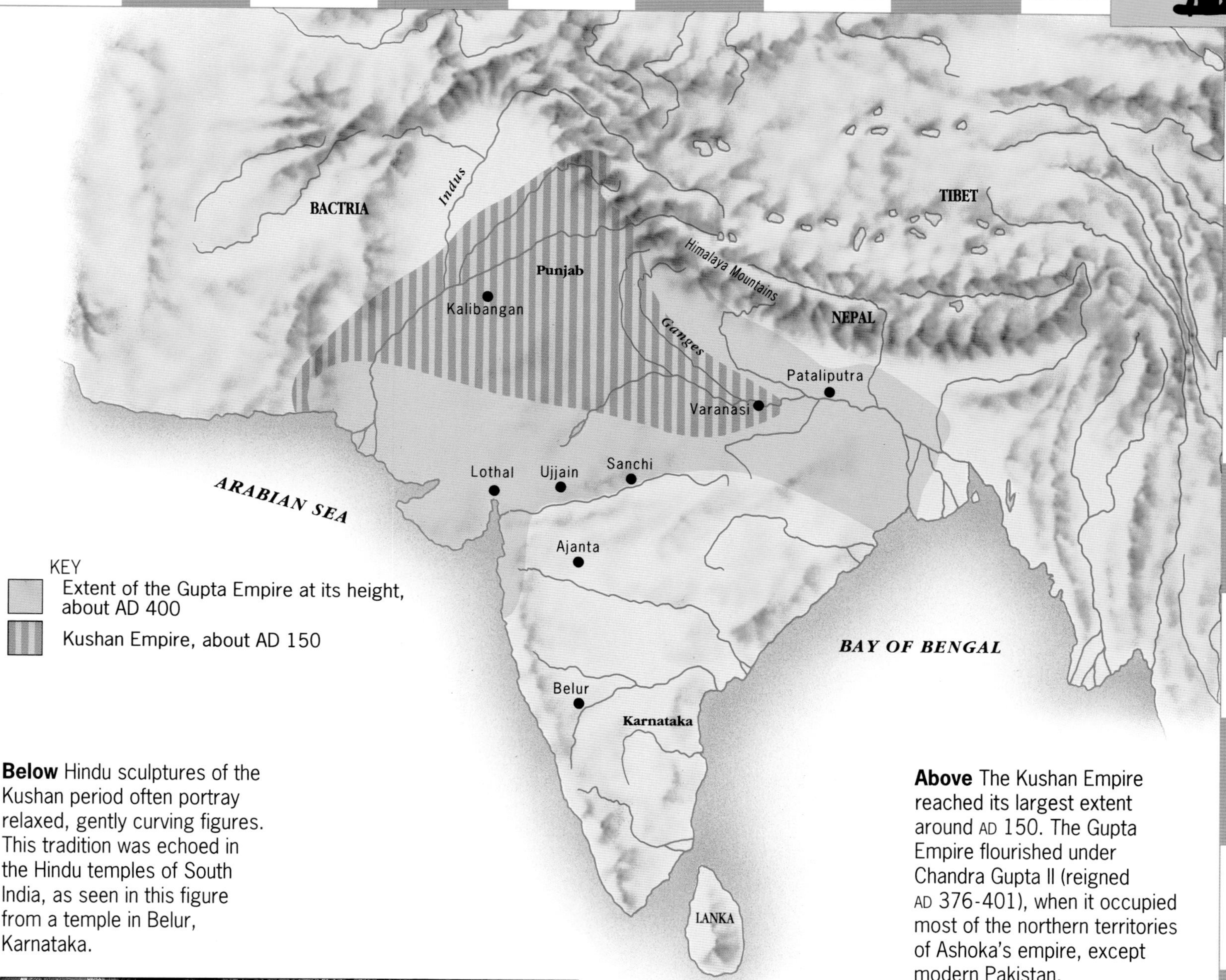

BACTRIA

Indus

Punjab

Kalibangan

TIBET

Himalaya Mountains

NEPAL

Ganges

Pataliputra

Varanasi

Lothal

Ujjain

Sanchi

ARABIAN SEA

Ajanta

BAY OF BENGAL

Belur

Karnataka

LANKA

KEY

Extent of the Gupta Empire at its height, about AD 400

Kushan Empire, about AD 150

Above The Kushan Empire reached its largest extent around AD 150. The Gupta Empire flourished under Chandra Gupta II (reigned AD 376-401), when it occupied most of the northern territories of Ashoka's empire, except modern Pakistan.

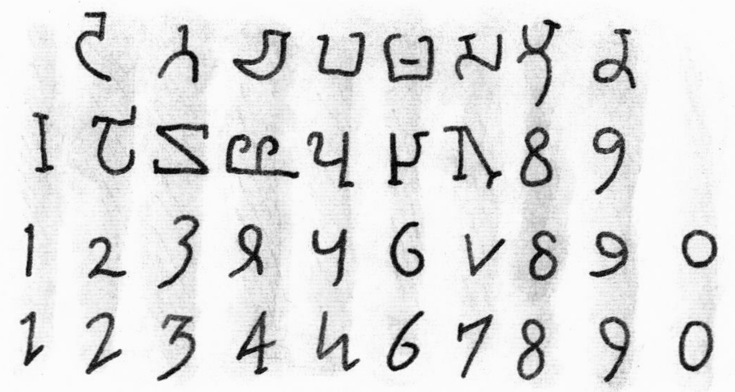

Below Hindu sculptures of the Kushan period often portray relaxed, gently curving figures. This tradition was echoed in the Hindu temples of South India, as seen in this figure from a temple in Belur, Karnataka.

Starting at zero

Indian mathematicians were using a number system based on ten by about 200 BC, and by AD 300 they had added the idea of zero. This method of counting was embraced in Alexandria (see pages 42-43) and formed the basis of the Arabic system of counting. Europe used Roman numerals until the 15th century, after which it switched to using Arabic numerals, which made calculating much simpler.

EMPIRES OF SOUTHEAST ASIA

With China to the north and India to the west, Southeast Asia has occupied a key trading position since ancient times.

Traders from India brought Hinduism to the region about the 1st century AD. Hinduism appealed to local rulers because of its system of laws, its ordered structure of society divided into castes, and the divine role that it gave to kings. The philosophy of Buddhism was brought by missionaries from India a couple of centuries later.

The Khmers, who dominated the region, founded their Hindu (later Buddhist) empire around AD 550. They built a magnificent capital at Angkor, but this was abandoned in the 15th century when the Khmers were overwhelmed by the rival Thai Empire.

Meanwhile the islands and sea-lanes to the south were controlled by the Buddhist Sailendra Empire based on Java. From the 13th century on, Islam—also brought by Indian traders—began to take hold on the coasts and islands, and the last Hindu empire of Java collapsed in 1515.

Ganesha—elephant of good fortune

Although the three main gods - Brahma, Vishnu, and Shiva - are widely recognized as the most important, many Hindus prefer to honor one of their other gods. This partly explains the success of Hinduism in Southeast Asia. Local gods could take their place in temples beside the Hindu gods from India. The most popular god from India was probably the elephant-headed Ganesha, the son of Shiva and the bringer of good fortune.

Left The Hindu kings of central Java built a huge temple complex at Prambanan, dating from the 9th century. The buildings are mainly ornate monuments called candis (pronounced "chandies"), to be viewed from the outside only, as were many of the early Indian Hindu temples. There were once over 200 candis on this site, but they were badly damaged by an earthquake in 1600. Some, however, have been restored. The main candi is dedicated to Shiva. Like many of the candis, it also contained the remains of a dead king, for Hindu kings were considered to be directly connected to the gods.

Above The people of Bali are still devoutly Hindu, and practice traditional Hindu rites - such as public cremation which, they believe, allows the dead to enter the spirit world. (The bodies here are inside the animal effigies, which are about to be set on fire.) Bali is now the only mainly Hindu island of Indonesia. The reason for this goes back to the 16th century. In 1515 the Majapahit empire, the last Hindu empire of Java, collapsed under pressure from new Islamic states. The rulers fled to the neighboring island of Bali, where they were able to preserve their Hindu traditions more or less undisturbed.

Right A Buddhist empire developed in Burma in the 9th century and spread along the valley of the Irrawaddy River. From 1044 its capital was the splendid city of Pagan. In 1287, however, Pagan was destroyed by Mongols from China under the direction of Kublai Khan (see pages 74-75). Now all that remains are hundreds of stupas—domed Buddhist shrines—most of them in ruins.

Below The 2000-year-old Shwedagon Pagoda dominates not only the surrounding temple complex but the whole city of Rangoon, capital of Burma. This vast, bell-shaped stupa (seen on the left of the picture) is said to contain hairs of the Buddha. To its full height of 330 feet (100 m), it is encrusted with layers of pure gold leaf, and the top contains thousands of jewels.

Above Huge stone statues of the Buddha can still be seen among the ruins of Sukhothai in Thailand. This was the capital of the Thai Empire from about 1228 to 1350.

Pagan
BURMA
Rangoon
THAILAND
Sukhothai
Angkor
INDOCHINA
SUMATRA
INDONESIA
JAVA
Prambanan
BALI

KEY

Khmer Empire

Srivijaya Empire

Sailendra Empire

Left Southeast Asia can be divided into two distinct parts: the mainland, attached to Asia, which is sometimes known as Indochina; and the many islands to the south. The empires tended to follow this division, vying with others within their own region, but seldom crossing the divide.

THE MOGULS

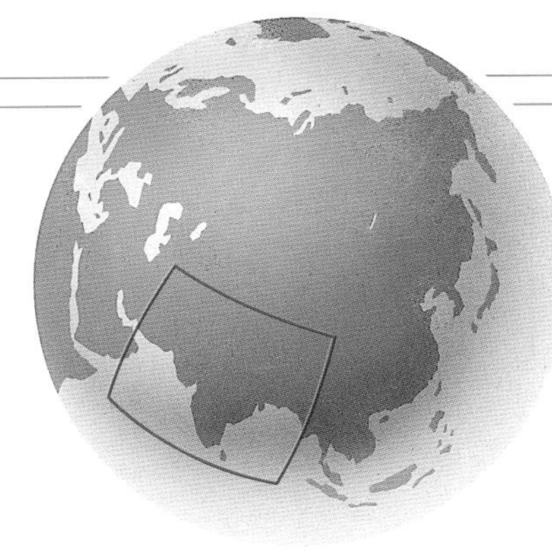

Below From paintings, as well as reports by foreign visitors, we know that Akbar's court was one of the most splendid, colorful and sophisticated of its day. This joyous painting of about 1561 shows the court celebrating the marriage of Akbar's sister.

In 1526 a descendant of Tamerlane, the last of the Mongolian Timurid rulers (see pages 74-75), invaded India from Afghanistan, defeated the Sultan of Delhi, and conquered most of northern India. He was Babur (1483-1530), a conqueror, ruler, and poet, and the founder of the Muslim Empire of the Moguls.

Babur's grandson, Akbar (reigned 1556-1605), extended the empire to include Afghanistan and parts of central and eastern India. Under Akbar, Muslim Indian art and architecture—a mixture of Persian and Indian traditions—reached its greatest peak. Akbar, who invited holy men of all religions to Fatehpur Sikri to discuss their beliefs, concluded that no religion should attempt to dominate another. In this way, as well as by creating an efficient administration, he was able to unite the diverse peoples of his empire.

This tradition was continued by his successors, Jehangir (reigned 1605-1627) and Shah Jahan (1628-1658). Aurangzeb (reigned 1658-1710) took the throne by ousting his father, Shah Jahan, and was far less liberal. Aurangzeb wanted to reassert strict Muslim values, and so dispensed with the tolerance of the Mogul court, and its painters. During his reign, the empire expanded to its greatest size. In the 18th century the empire broke up into squabbling provinces. The British took full advantage of this situation when they carved out an empire in India for themselves. However, they kept the Mogul Empire alive in name until 1857.

Beautiful memorial

The Taj Mahal in Agra is a magnificent tomb built by Emperor Shah Jahan for his wife Mumtaz-i-Mahal, who died in 1629. It was designed by a Turkish architect, and craftsmen from France and Italy were brought in to help with its construction. The white marble walls are decorated with patterns of semi-precious stone.

Mogul art

Babur commissioned artists to paint the plants and animals of his new empire, beginning a tradition among the Mogul emperors. Jehangir's favorite artist, Mansur, painted birds and flowers, usually directly from nature. His style was influenced by Renaissance painters (see pages 60-61) and European scientific illustrations.

Left About 1580 Akbar built a magnificent royal city at Fatehpur Sikri—a great monument to Mogul architecture. Unfortunately, there was not enough water for the city. Two years after Akbar's death in 1605 the city was abandoned, and has remained deserted to this day.

Below The Mogul emperors generally tolerated other religions. The Sikh religion, which combines Hinduism and Islam, follows the teachings of its founder, Guru Nanak (1469-1539). The holiest shrine of the Sikhs is the Golden Temple at Amritsar.

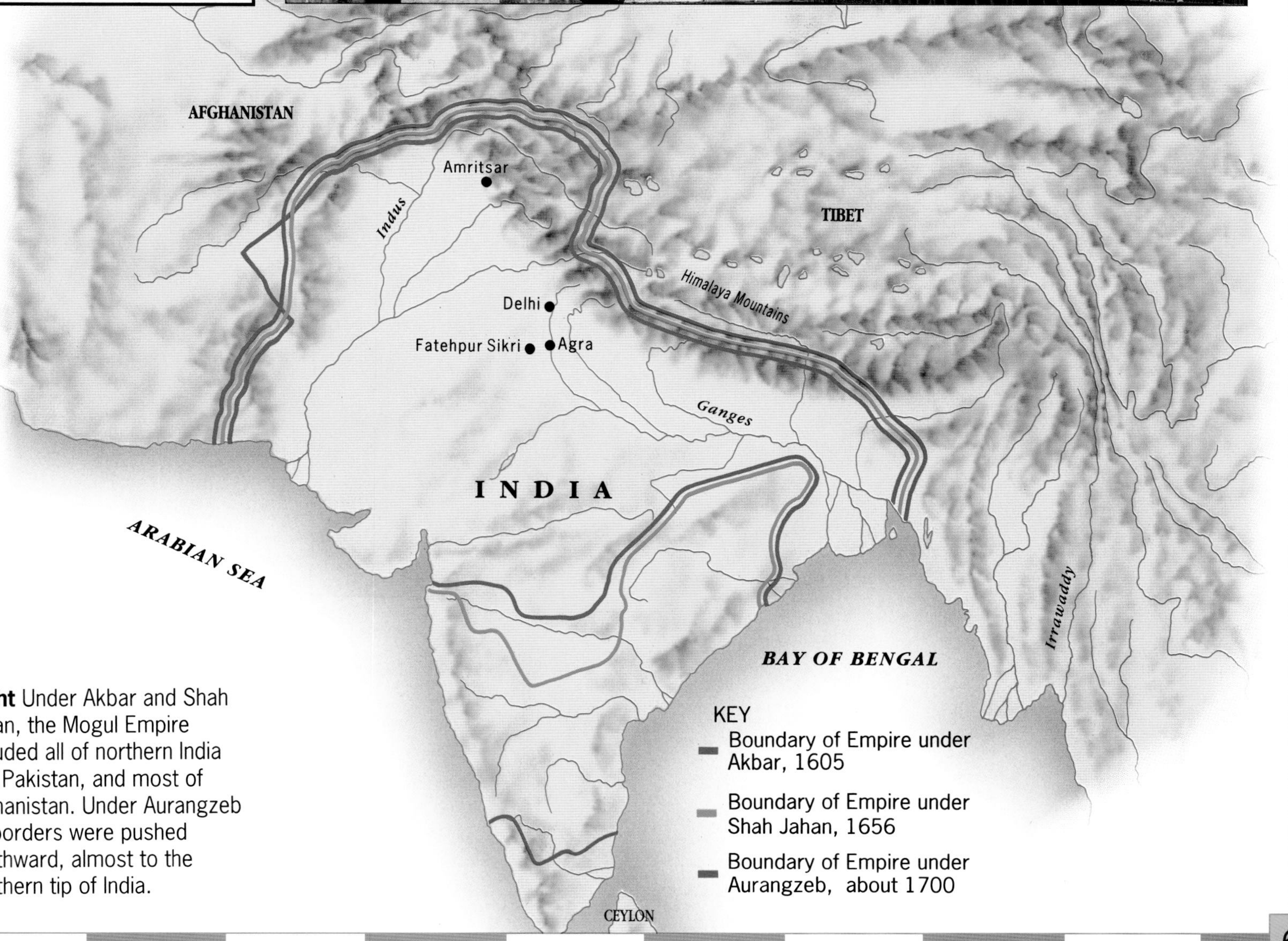

AFGHANISTAN
Amritsar
Indus
TIBET
Delhi
Himalaya Mountains
Fatehpur Sikri
Agra
Ganges
INDIA
ARABIAN SEA
BAY OF BENGAL
Irrawaddy
CEYLON

KEY
Boundary of Empire under Akbar, 1605
Boundary of Empire under Shah Jahan, 1656
Boundary of Empire under Aurangzeb, about 1700

Right Under Akbar and Shah Jahan, the Mogul Empire included all of northern India and Pakistan, and most of Afghanistan. Under Aurangzeb its borders were pushed southward, almost to the southern tip of India.

SECTION 7: EAST ASIA

Strong philosophies and moral codes that emphasized harmony and good behavior molded the civilizations of the Far East. The search for stability led to long periods of isolation from the rest of the world, frequently disrupted by turmoil and warfare.

CHINA UNDER THE ZHOU AND HAN DYNASTIES

The rule of the Zhou Dynasty in China (about 1122-256 BC) is known as the "Classical Age." Although often a troubled period, it produced two philosophers who had a lasting influence. Confucius (about 551-479 BC) advocated a code of behavior based on the importance of goodness. Lao-Tzu (604-531 BC) is the semi-legendary founder of Taoism. He taught that the most important thing in life was to find Tao, which means "The Way" — the harmony of nature which gives rise to the right way of behaving in all situations in life.

Iron became widely used in China about 700 BC, and was put to use during the troubled Warring States period (475-221 BC) in weapons and in tools to build extensive canals for transportation and irrigation. China was united under the Qin or Ch'in Dynasty (221-206 BC), and the Dynasty's founder, Qin Shi Huangdi, (reigned 221-210 BC) became the first emperor.

Under the Han Dynasty (202 BC-AD 220) the empire was extended into Vietnam and Korea. During this period of stable rule, central government was administered by civil servants, who were chosen for their ability by a system of exams. Military and diplomatic expeditions in the Far West made contact with the edge of the Western world for the first time, paving the way for the Silk Roads, which carried Far Eastern goods across Asia for the next 1,500 years.

The Great Wall

A number of sections of the Great Wall of China were already in existence when they were joined into a single wall by Emperor Qin around 210 BC. This task took nine years, and involved about a million laborers. Many were convicts, and thousands died in the effort. The intention was to create a defendable wall to prevent raiding tribes, such as the Hsiung Nu (Huns), from entering China.

The Great Wall has a number of walls branching off it, all of which once added up to a total length of about 4,000 miles (6,400 km). About two thirds is still standing, although most of what is left dates from rebuilding during the Ming Dynasty (AD 1368-1644).

Left In ancient times, slaves and courtiers were buried alive with a dead Chinese king, to serve him and protect him in the afterlife. This was no longer the practice in Emperor Qin's time. Instead over 7,000 life-size clay soldiers and horses were made, and these were buried with the emperor in a vast tomb, measuring 3 miles (5 km) across, at Xi'an, central China. This strange "Terracotta Army" remained hidden and forgotten until the tomb was accidentally rediscovered in 1974. The huge task of excavating the site is still going on.

Easy arithmetic

The abacus is an ancient Chinese calculating machine, dating back to about 500 BC. It is essentially an adding machine, but can also be used for subtraction, multiplication, and division. The abacus is still widely used in small businesses and shops today. Skilled operators can perform complex calculations with remarkable speed.

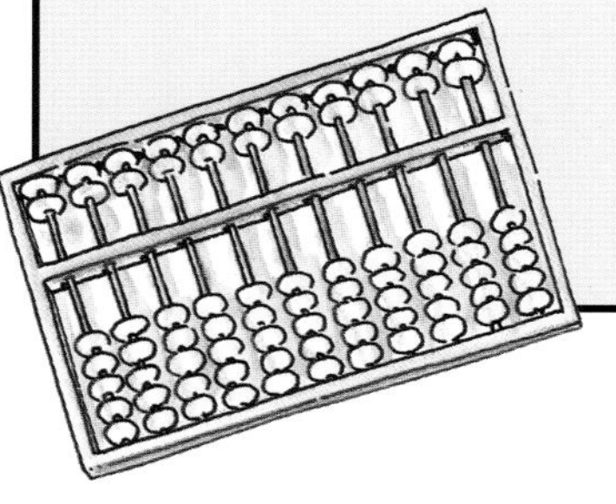

Right The Chinese were gifted horsemen, and horses have always featured prominently in their art and sculpture, as in this rubbing from a Han Dynasty tomb decoration. The native horses were fairly small, so when Emperor Han Wu-ti (141-87 BC) heard about the larger horses of Western Asia, he waged a campaign in the extreme west of China to capture as many as possible.

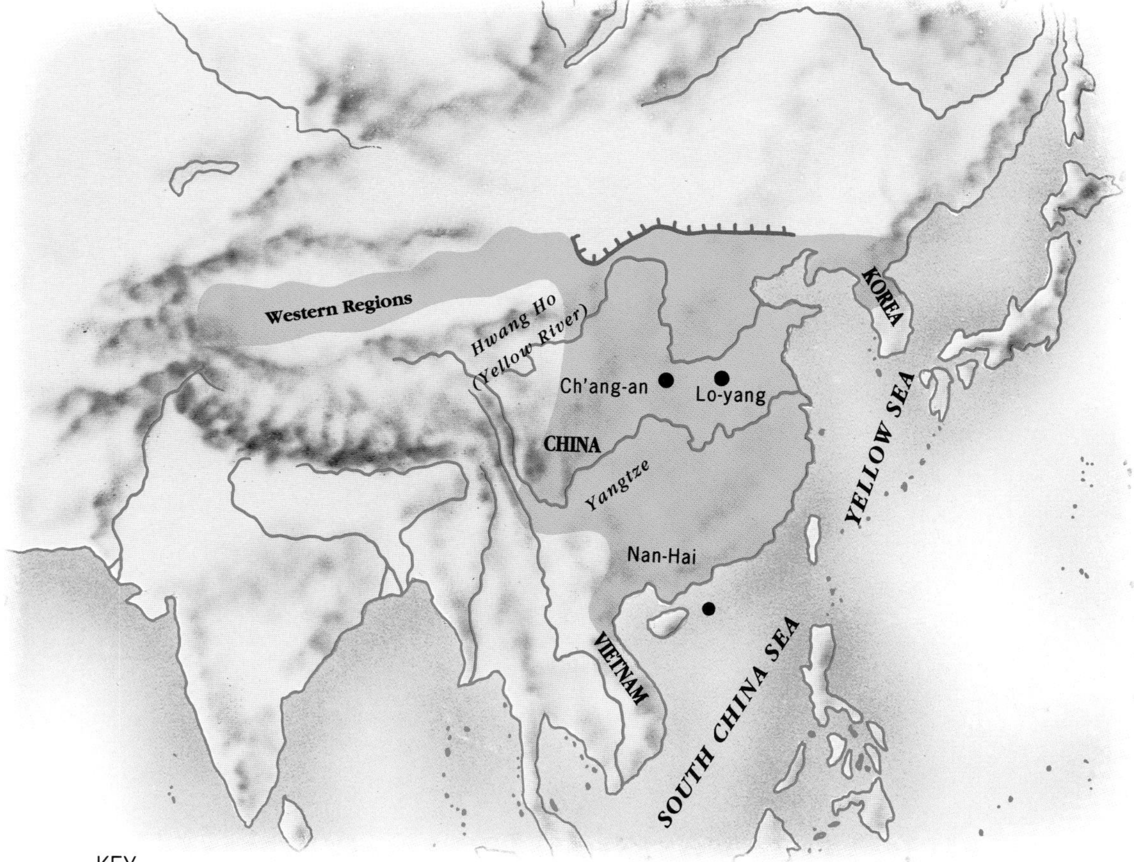

Right During the Han Dynasty, the Chinese Empire reached its greatest extent of ancient times. The Great Wall extended along much of the northern border. The territories stretching westward into Central Asia provided a corridor to the western world that formed the basis of the Silk Roads.

CHINA UNDER THE TANG AND SONG DYNASTIES

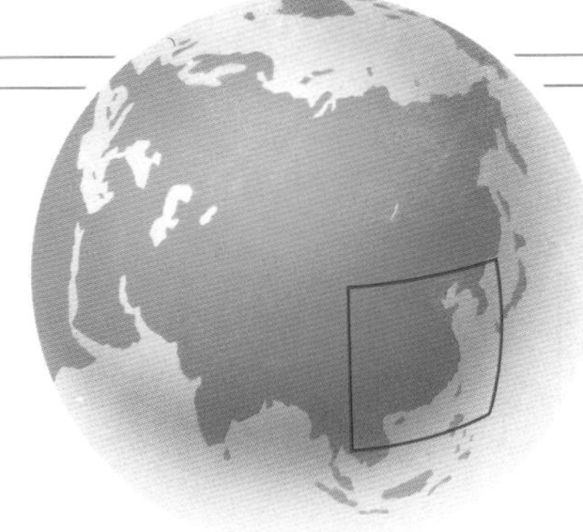

China's history repeats a pattern of prosperity, unity, and stability, followed by disintegration, revolt, and invasion. Nearly 400 years of turmoil followed the Han Dynasty, as the empire split up into the Three Kingdoms (AD 220-65), then was briefly reunited under the Tsin Dynasty (AD 265-420), before being invaded by nomads in AD 316.

Under the Sui Dynasty (AD 581-618) China was again reunified. The Great Wall was repaired and the canal system extended. This was a time of important change. Buddhism was beginning to take hold, and Taoism gained in importance. It laid the foundations for the Tang Dynasty (AD 618-907), a "Golden Age" during which the empire stretched from Korea to Turkestan. Taizong (reigned AD 627-649), one of the great emperors of China, reintroduced the Confucian system of selecting highly trained government officials through examinations. In this way, in principle at least, the administration was run by the most gifted men of the land.

A period of warfare followed under the Five Dynasties and Ten Kingdoms (AD 907-960), but the Song Dynasty (AD 960-1279) brought an era of renewed prosperity. It was a time of great inventiveness, in mining, cast-iron technology, and pottery. An important invention was movable type, and this led to printed books and newspapers, and even paper money.

This period came to a sudden and dramatic close with another invasion, this time by the Mongols (see pages 74-75).

China

Chinese potters developed extremely delicate forms of pottery, such as celadon (left) and porcelain. Chinese pottery later became so famous that all fine pottery became known in English as "china."

Left The Tang Dynasty was noted in particular for its distinctive *sancai* ("three-color") pottery. The three colors were green, cream, and brown, but black was used as well. These figures were beautifully moulded, and the glaze, by contrast, seems rather crude. Because sancai pieces were often placed in tombs, a large number of them have survived.

Above Buddhism reached China around the 1st century AD, but it did not really catch on until the 6th century. After that it spread quickly. Missionaries and monks traveled along the Silk Roads, and Buddhist temples and monasteries were built throughout much of the empire. Many people continued to follow Confucianism, Taoism, and traditional ancestor worship, and simply adopted aspects of Buddhism as well.

Right Tea was grown in China in prehistoric times, but after the 8th century AD it was grown in large quantities and sold as a commercial crop. Tea was introduced to Europe in the 17th century, and has since become the world's second most widely-consumed drink after water.

Below Chinese painting of the Song Dynasty (AD 960-1279) was remarkably sophisticated compared with art of the same period which came from other parts of the world.

Right Gunpowder was invented by the Chinese in the 9th century, but for a long time it was used only to make fireworks. During the Song Dynasty, however, it was used in various kinds of weapons of war such as rockets, bombs and "rushing-out-fire-guns" — bamboo tubes filled with gunpowder which fired bullets. Gunpowder was first used in Europe in the 14th century.

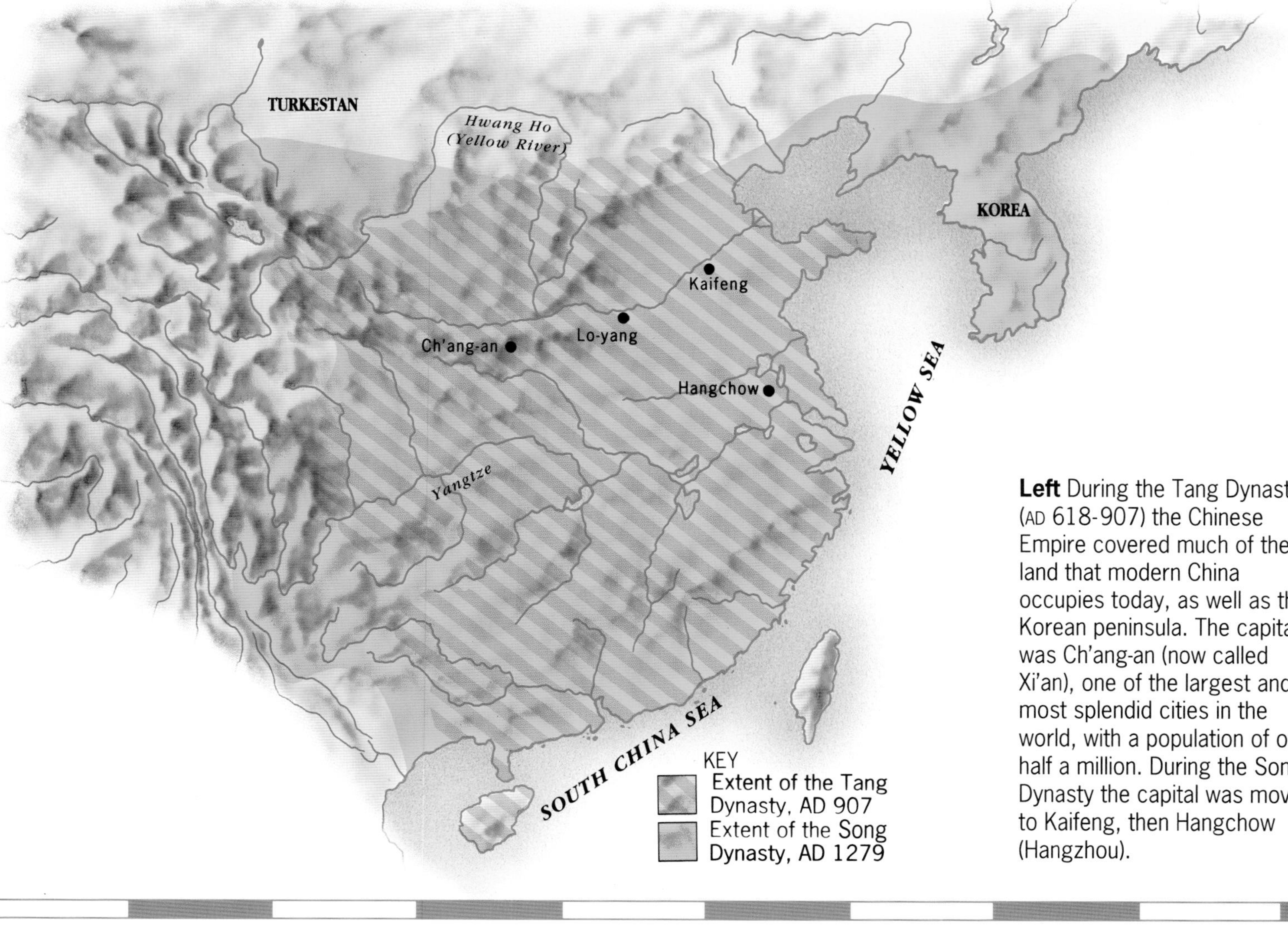

TURKESTAN
Hwang Ho (Yellow River)
KOREA
Kaifeng
Lo-yang
Ch'ang-an
Hangchow
YELLOW SEA
Yangtze
SOUTH CHINA SEA
KEY
Extent of the Tang Dynasty, AD 907
Extent of the Song Dynasty, AD 1279

Left During the Tang Dynasty (AD 618-907) the Chinese Empire covered much of the land that modern China occupies today, as well as the Korean peninsula. The capital was Ch'ang-an (now called Xi'an), one of the largest and most splendid cities in the world, with a population of over half a million. During the Song Dynasty the capital was moved to Kaifeng, then Hangchow (Hangzhou).

THE MONGOLS

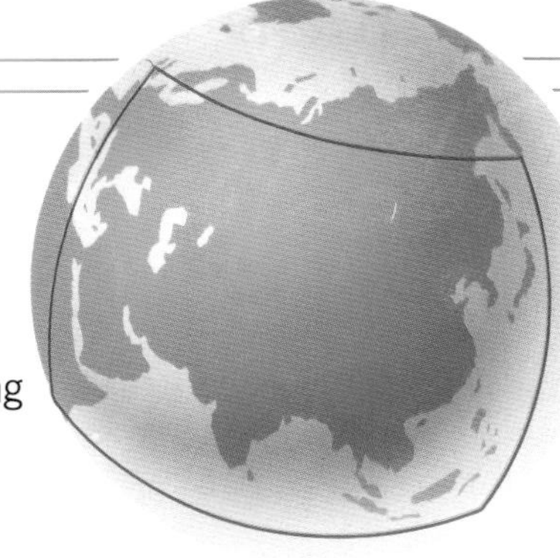

China had always feared the nomadic peoples who lived in the harsh, mountainous landscape beyond their borders to the north and who regularly poured over the Great Wall to attack them. In the early 13th century the Mongolian tribes were united by Genghis Khan (about 1162-1227) to create a powerful nation, centering on their capital, Karakorum. In 1213-1215 they swept into China, and then headed across Asia, reaching the borders of Europe in 1224. Genghis Khan was one of the greatest conquerors the world has ever known.

After Genghis Khan's death, the empire continued to expand rapidly. In 1260 Kublai Khan, a grandson of Genghis, took over the Great Khanate, which comprised the whole of China. But by now it no longer held power over the other khanates. The Kipchak Khanate in Russia, founded by another of Genghis's grandsons, Batu Khan, was famous for its magnificent camp on the banks of the Volga River, and was called the Empire of the Golden Horde.

In 1368 the Mongols were expelled from China. But Timur, or Tamerlane (about 1336-1405), a Mongol ruler from Samarkand, now attempted to reconquer the old Mongolian Empire. He invaded Persia, the Empire of the Golden Horde, and northern India, and attacked the Ottoman Empire in Asia Minor. He founded the Timurid Dynasty, which made Samarkand a center of Muslim civilization and led directly to the Mogul Empire in India (see pages 68-69).

Below The Mongols were fearsome warriors, who used their great skills as horsemen to mount quick and devastating attacks. This painting of 1548 shows Timur's army attacking a town.

West meets East

During the Mongol era, trade continued along the Silk Roads. It was conducted by a series of middlemen, and few merchants ever completed the whole journey themselves. The first recorded European merchants to travel to China were two brothers called Polo. In 1271 they took a young son, Marco, with them (seen here leaving from Venice). He spent a total of 17 years in China and came back deeply impressed by its immense riches and the sophistication of its civilization.

Above Marco Polo was well received at the court of Kublai Khan (above). The emperor made him ambassador, and he traveled widely all over the Chinese Empire, making reports on what he saw.

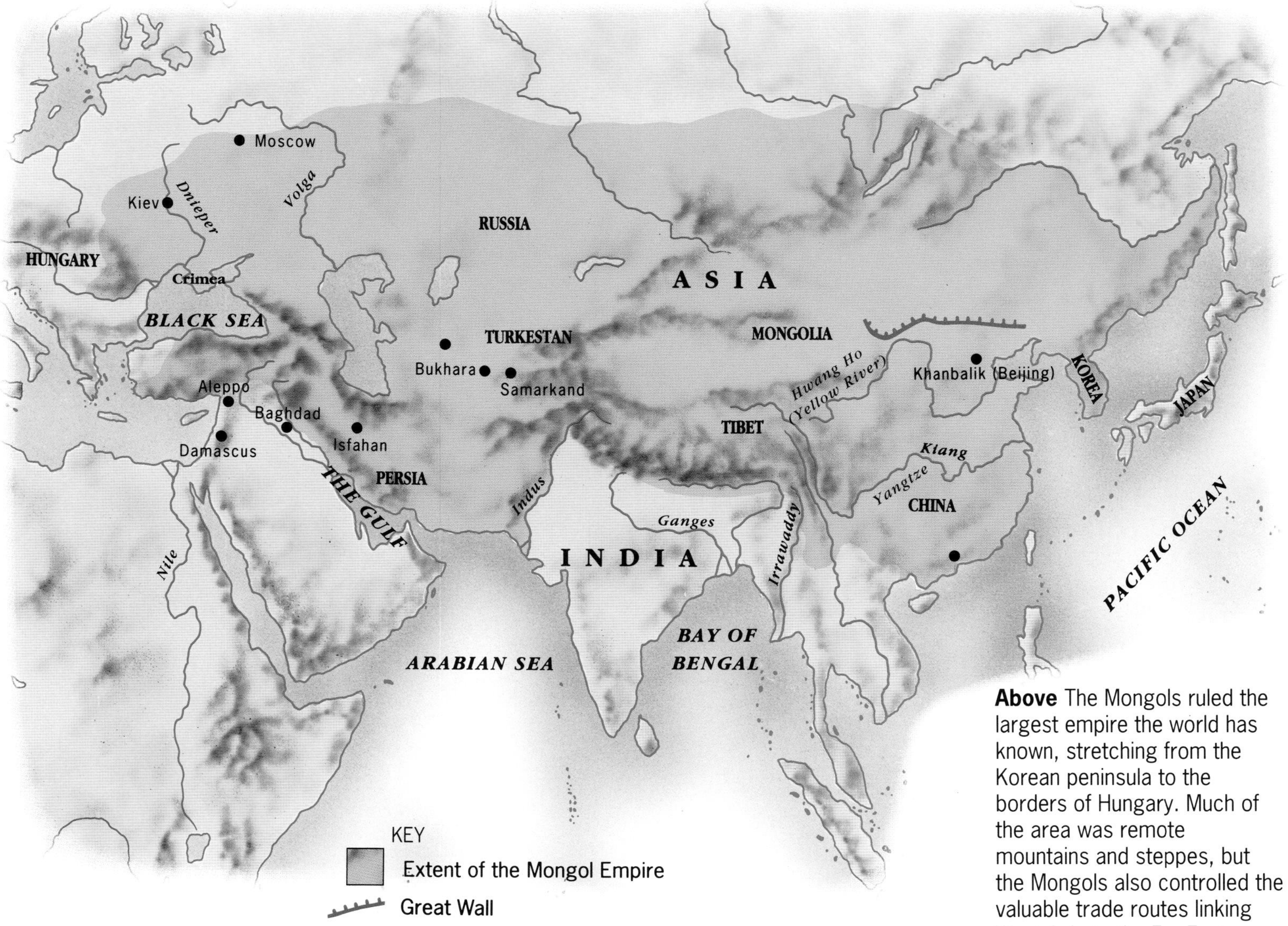

Moscow
Kiev
Dnieper
Volga
RUSSIA
HUNGARY
Crimea
BLACK SEA
ASIA
TURKESTAN
MONGOLIA
Bukhara
Samarkand
Hwang Ho (Yellow River)
Khanbalik (Beijing)
KOREA
JAPAN
Aleppo
Baghdad
Damascus
Isfahan
PERSIA
THE GULF
TIBET
Kiang
Yangtze
CHINA
PACIFIC OCEAN
Indus
Ganges
INDIA
Irrawaddy
Nile
ARABIAN SEA
BAY OF BENGAL

KEY
Extent of the Mongol Empire
Great Wall

Above The Mongols ruled the largest empire the world has known, stretching from the Korean peninsula to the borders of Hungary. Much of the area was remote mountains and steppes, but the Mongols also controlled the valuable trade routes linking West Asia to the Far East.

Gruesome monuments

The Mongols were feared by the Islamic World and the Europeans. They slaughtered their enemies mercilessly, and built pyramids of skulls on the battlefield. When Hulagu Khan (1217-1265) destroyed Baghdad in 1258, a million people died.

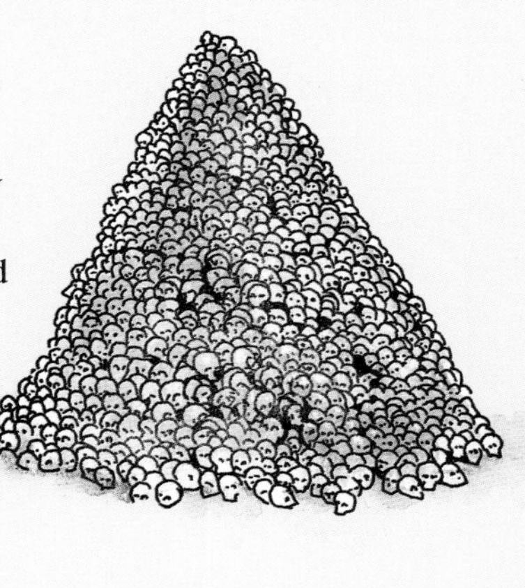

Left Kublai Khan was the first Chinese emperor to make his capital in Beijing, which was known then as Khanbalik. This gilded head is from the Forbidden City, the emperor's court, built during the Ming Dynasty (1368-1644).

Right The Mongols took their traditional felt tents, called yurts, with them on their campaigns. Such tents are still used by the nomadic herders of Mongolia.

JAPAN AND KOREA

The histories of both Korea and Japan are closely linked to their powerful neighbor, China. Korea was invaded by China in 108 BC, and three independent Chinese-style kingdoms followed. In the 7th century AD the Silla Kingdom brought the whole peninsula under its rule, until the Sui and Tang dynasties of China invaded (see pages 72-73). The Koryo Dynasty ruled from 935 AD until the Mongol invasions (see pages 74-75). After 1392 the Yi Dynasty made its capital at Hanyang (now Seoul), adopted a Confucian style of government, and survived until 1910.

Japan was unified in the 5th century under the Yamato clan, who set up a Chinese-style emperor's court at Nara. Buddhism and Confucianism were introduced and existed alongside Shinto, the traditional form of ancestor worship.

Now Japan became an increasingly feudal state of competing warlords, assisted by the samurai. These warriors were the power behind Minamoto no Yoritomo (1147-1199), who became the first shogun (military dictator) in 1192, and founded the Kamakura Shogunate (1185-1333).

Below The nobles of the Silla Kingdom were buried beneath huge mounds of earth, which can still be seen at their capital of Kyongju, South Korea. Their tombs also contained jewelry made of gold and jade, pottery, sculpture, and weapons.

A period of civil war resulted in unification in 1600 under Tokugawa Ieyasu (1542-1616), who founded the Tokugawa Shogunate (1603-1867). He suppressed the Christians, whose numbers had increased rapidly after the arrival of European missionaries in the 1540s, and cut Japan off from the outside world. His clan ruled for 250 years, when Japanese culture flourished in isolation.

Left The Heian Period was named after Heian-hyo (now Kyoto), which was the capital of Japan from AD 794 to 1868. One of its most famous buildings is the Golden Pavilion, so named because the upper stories are covered in gold leaf. It was built in 1397 as a retreat for Shogun Ashikaga Yoshimitsu, who practiced the Japanese form of Buddhism called Zen. After his death it became a Zen Buddhist temple. The building seems to be in tune with Heian-hyo's name, which means "Capital of Peace and Tranquillity." In fact Heian-hyo's history was far from tranquil, and it was repeatedly raided by the samurai. The Golden Pavilion survived until 1950, when it was set on fire by a mentally disturbed monk. A precise replica was built in its place in 1955.

Samurai skills

The samurai were a warrior elite, similar in many ways to the knights of feudal Europe (see pages 58-59). They were highly trained and well-armed. Many samurai were also gifted poets and painters.

Left Tea was introduced to Japan from China, especially during the Chinese Tang Dynasty (AD 618-907). Zen Buddhists believed that tea helped them to meditate. During the Ashikaga Period (1392-1573) tea drinking developed into a stylized ceremony, and often took place in a specially constructed building. It involved an elaborate ritual, during which various teas were prepared by the host and served with light snacks.

Left Lacquerwork was one of the most beautiful of the Japanese crafts. It dates back to at least the 2nd century BC, but reached the height of sophistication during the Ashikaga Period. Objects were decorated with up to 30 layers of lacquer (a tree resin) and then painted, or decorated with gold dust and gold leaf.

Above From the 1st century to the 7th century AD the kings and nobles of Japan were also buried beneath tumuli mounds, in tombs filled with treasure and artifacts. This pottery head is from a tomb of the 6th century AD.

Below The most important influence on the cultures of Korea and Japan was China. However, their geographical positions in relation to China show why each was able to develop its own distinctive form of civilization. Unlike Korea, Japan was never ruled directly by the Chinese.

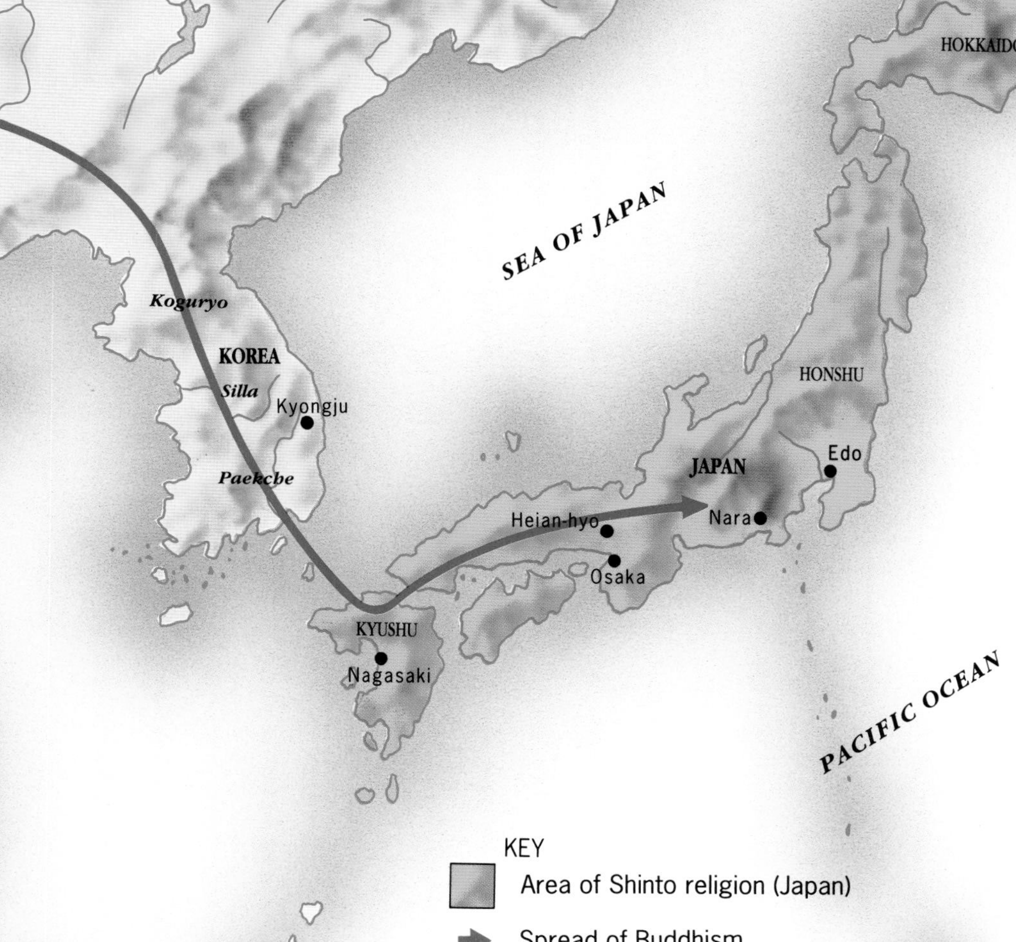

SECTION 8: THE AMERICAS

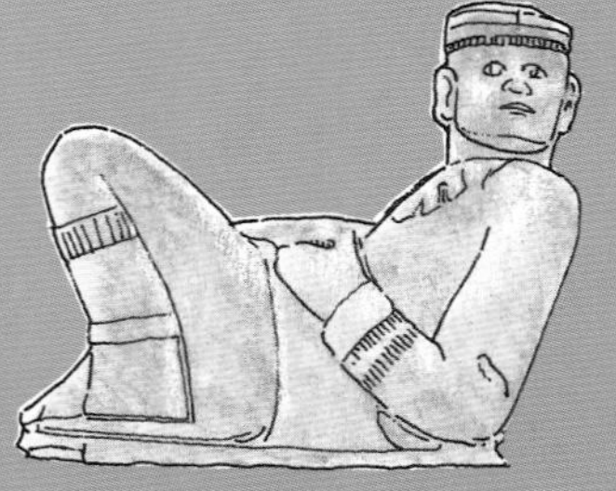

The civilizations of the Americas were isolated from the rest of the world, but followed the same pattern. Town-building cultures emerged from settled farming communities. When the Europeans arrived, they easily overwhelmed the American cultures, which were still in the Bronze Age.

EARLY NORTH AMERICAN CULTURES

The first people in North America may have arrived 50,000 years ago by crossing a neck of land that joined Alaska to Asia. After 12,000 BC they moved south and spread out across the Great Plains as nomadic hunter-gatherers.

Cliff-dwellers

Canyon de Chelly, Arizona, has been inhabited for over 2,000 years—the longest continuously inhabited place in North America. Some of the spectacular ruins date back to AD 350. The earliest inhabitants built houses of adobe-brick or lived in the caves, and grew corn in the river valley. Stone buildings, some of them over six stories high, were constructed after the development of the Pueblo civilization in about AD 1000.

Pueblo Indians were settled farmers; they made cotton cloth, jewelry from turquoise, and distinctive pottery. Their lands were raided by Athabascan-speaking peoples, ancestors of the Apache and Navajo. Canyon de Chelly is now part of the Navajo homeland.

By about 2000 BC hunters in the Great Plains were using bows and arrows to pursue buffalo, and making clothes and tents with the skins.

In the southwest, people of the Cochise culture were growing corn by 2000 BC. In the eastern woodlands, the Delaware, Huron, and Iroquois hunted deer, grew corn and beans, lived in wigwams and wooden villages, and made canoes out of birchbark.

On the northwest Pacific coast the Chinook and Kwakiutl lived by salmon-fishing and hunting, while in the far north, Aleuts and the Inuit (or Eskimos) survived in one of the world's harshest environments by seasonal hunting and fishing.

The horse was introduced to North America by the Spanish in the 16th century and the hunting cultures of the Blackfoot, Cheyenne, Comanche, Crow, and Sioux evolved.

But over the four centuries that followed the arrival of these and other Europeans, all the native American peoples were decimated by disease, the loss of their lands, and war.

Mound-builders

Between about 1000 BC and AD 1500 huge mounds were built by the Hopewell and Adena cultures, who lived in the valleys of the Ohio and Mississippi rivers. The tops of some of these mounds were decorated with earthworks in the form of animals or shapes, as at the Serpent Mound in Ohio. The mounds appear to have served a number of functions: the earlier ones were tombs; later ones had temples built on top.

Artifacts including sculptures and weapons have been found at these sites, which demonstrates that there were widespread trading links across North America. This copper bird (above) was found in a Hopewell burial mound.

Left Totem poles are carved and painted wooden sculptures, found particularly among the peoples of the northwest Pacific coast. They are mainly clan symbols, portraying characters and animals from myths, and ancestor figures. This Kwakiutl pole shows a mythological woman with her son.

Above Traditional Inuit art was applied to tools and weapons, and often shows scenes of hunting and fishing. This caribou hunt is engraved on a walrus tusk.

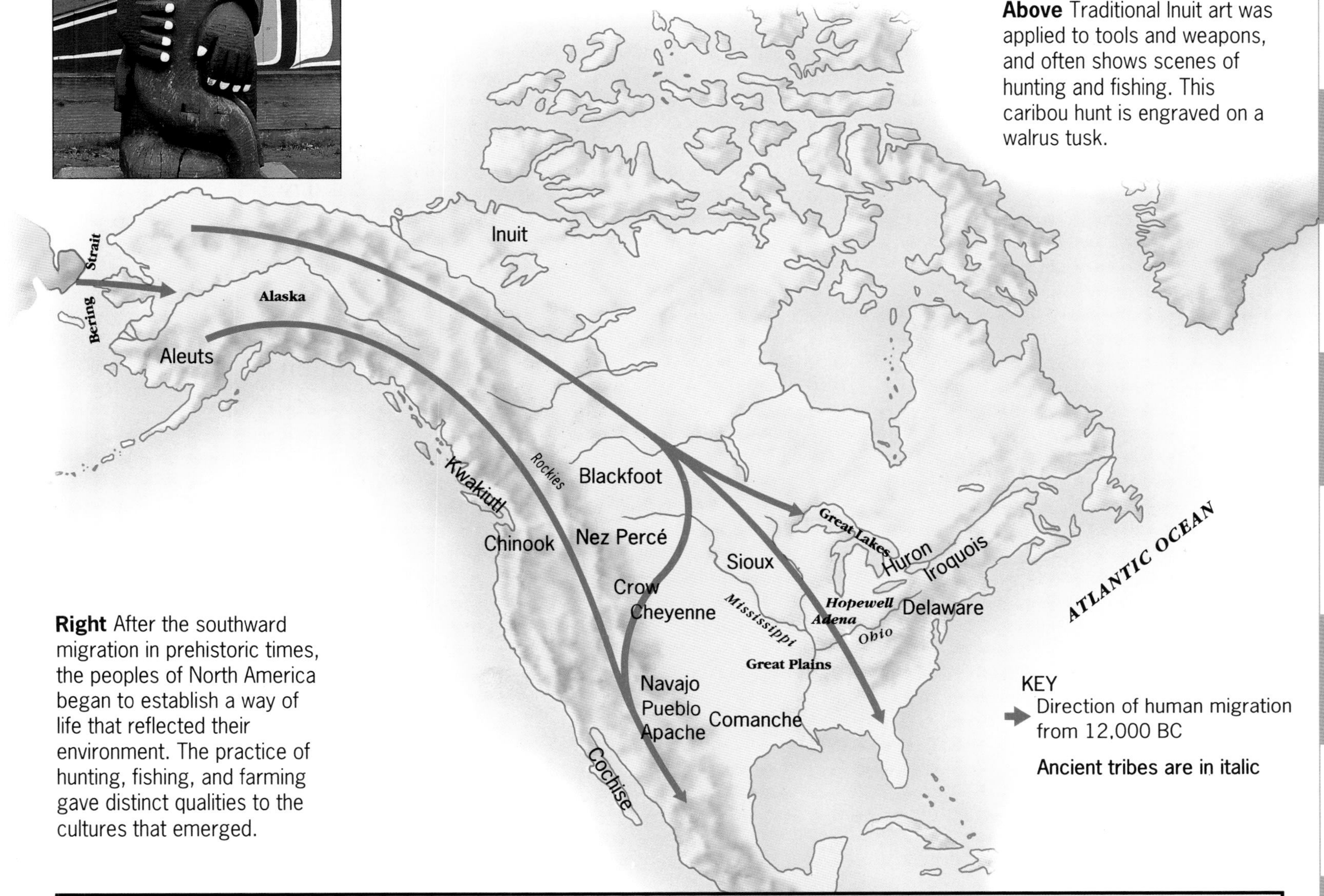

KEY
Direction of human migration from 12,000 BC
Ancient tribes are in italic

Right After the southward migration in prehistoric times, the peoples of North America began to establish a way of life that reflected their environment. The practice of hunting, fishing, and farming gave distinct qualities to the cultures that emerged.

Indian wars

Europeans began to settle in the east and southwest of North America in the 17th century. Many native American cultures altered through trade. The Nez Percé (right), for example, started to use firearms and horses for the first time. Conflict resulted in a series of wars as the new settlers spread out into the heart of North America in the 19th century.

THE OLMECS, MAYA, AND TOLTECS

The development of corn farming was the starting point for the great civilizations of Meso-America (Mexico and Central America) around 2500 BC. By 1500 BC farming was well-established and settled cultures grew up around temple sites. These later developed into magnificent temple-cities.

From around 1250 to 400 BC the agricultural society of the Olmecs dominated the eastern Mexican lowlands. The Olmecs are particularly known for the huge carved stone heads that they produced.

Meanwhile the Mayan civilization developed in the Yucatán, Guatemala, and western Honduras, reaching its peak after AD 300, when it dominated the region. The Maya were gifted astronomers and mathematicians; they used picture writing and had extremely accurate calendars. Quite suddenly, however, their cities were abandoned in the 9th century AD.

During this time other cultures had developed elsewhere, notably at Teotihuacán in central Mexico, which from the 1st to the 8th century AD had a population of over 100,000. The Toltecs dominated central Mexico after the fall of Teotihuacán in AD 900, ruling from their capital at Tollan (Tula). They also controlled much of the old Mayan lands. The Mayan and Toltec cultures gradually merged after about 1200, to create a second great Mayan period.

Above The huge Olmec stone heads weigh up to 40 tons. Since no ancient American used the wheel, they were probably transported to their sites by river craft.

Right Although the Olmecs had only Stone-Age technology, they were gifted sculptors.

By the time the Europeans arrived in the early 16th century the Maya had suffered over a century of decline and strife. The Toltecs, for their part, had been destroyed by the nomadic Chichimec people, paving the way for the rise of the Aztecs (see pages 82-83).

Temple-cities

Like many of the ancient cities of Meso-America, Palenque was dominated by its great pyramid-like structures. The Palace (left) stood on one of these. Another was a temple, and another contained the tomb of a great ruler named Pacal (reigned AD 615-683). No one knows why the Mayan cities were abandoned around AD 850.

Temples of time

Chichén Itzá was founded about AD 514. Unlike other Mayan cities, such as Palenque and Copán, most of the buildings date from the later Mayan era. The Temple of the Warriors (left) includes statues of the gods and hundreds of columns, which were once roofed over. *El Castillo* is a four-sided pyramid temple. The 91 steps on each side, plus the top, add up to 365, the number of days in the year. At the spring and autumn equinox a snakelike shadow is cast down the steps—an image of the snake-god Quetzalcoatl.

There was also an observatory at Chichén Itzá. Mayan religious ceremonies were held at precise times of the year. The calendar was based on exact astronomical observations.

Below Teotihuacán occupies a vast site, which includes two huge stepped pyramids as well as the Temple of Quetzalcoatl. The temple is decorated with sculptures of the feathered serpent Quetzalcoatl, later a central god of the Toltecs.

Below The boundaries of the Meso-American civilizations followed patterns that were dictated by the landscape, which varied from the dry lowlands of the Yucatán peninsula to the jungle-covered hills to the west.

Below The Maya played a game that involved putting a hard rubber ball through fixed stone hoops. The game had a religious function: it represented the battle between the forces of life and death.

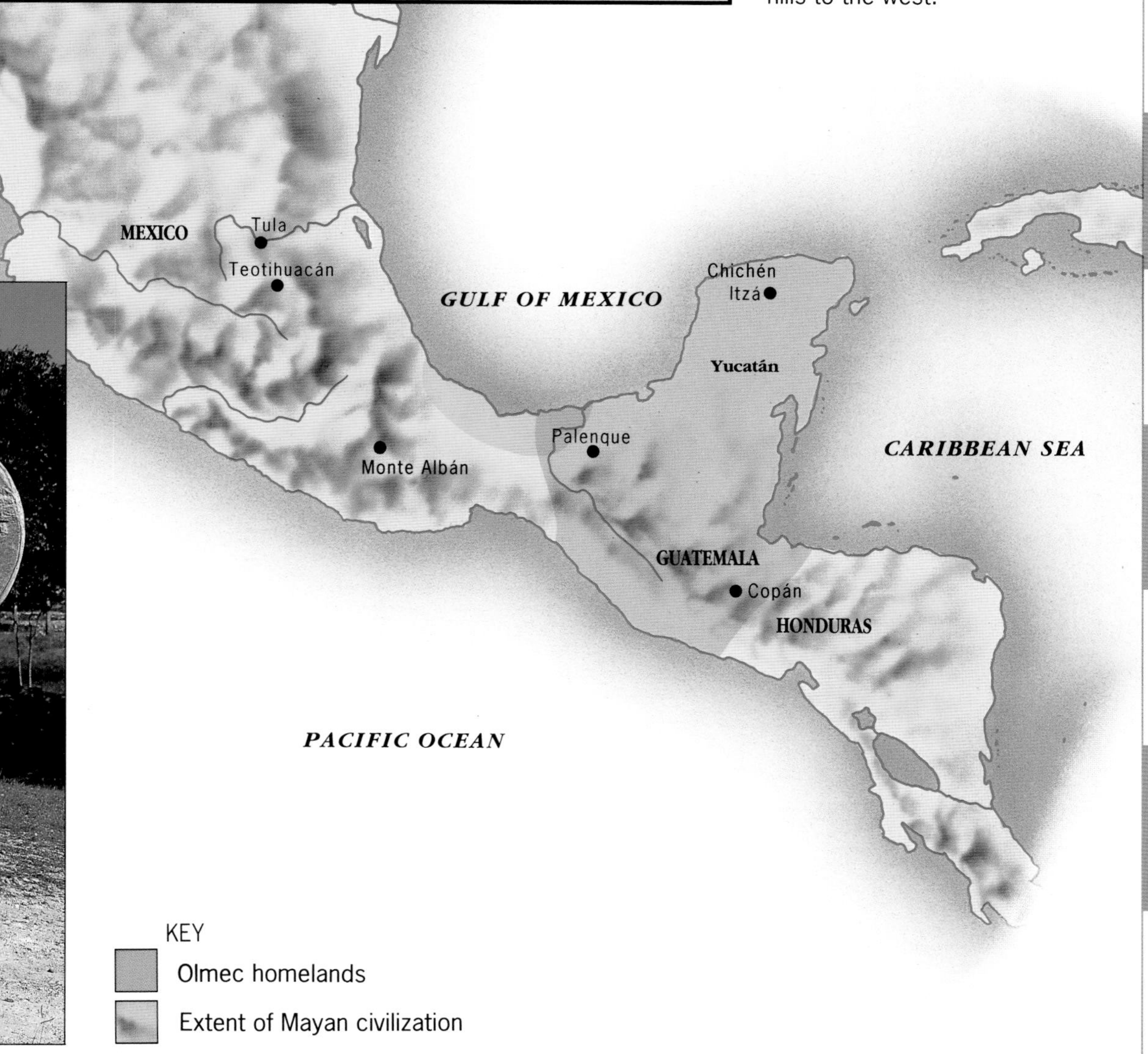

MEXICO
Tula
Teotihuacán
GULF OF MEXICO
Chichén Itzá
Yucatán
Palenque
Monte Albán
CARIBBEAN SEA
GUATEMALA
Copán
HONDURAS
PACIFIC OCEAN

KEY
Olmec homelands
Extent of Mayan civilization

THE AZTECS

The chaos that followed the collapse of the Toltecs was resolved by the Aztecs. This poor nomadic tribe rose to power in the mid-14th century by forging a series of alliances with more powerful neighbors. Their capital was Tenochtitlán (modern Mexico City), founded in about 1345 on Lake Texcoco, on a set of islands divided by canals. During the 15th century the Aztecs expanded their empire ruthlessly, conquering the Mixtecs and Zapotecs to the south and extending their boundaries across Meso-America. Their subjects had to pay them tribute of precious metals, jewels, decorative feathers, cocoa, rubber—as well as victims for human sacrifice. As a result, the Aztec rulers were bitterly resented throughout much of their empire.

The Aztecs built on centuries of achievement by the civilizations of Meso-America in such varied fields as building, irrigation, astronomy, mathematics, the arts, weaving, and sculpture. They recorded their religious practices, their history, and the administration of their empire in picture books called "codices," made of tree bark or agave leaves. By the 16th century Tenochtitlán, the most splendid of American cities, was the administrative and religious capital of the empire ruled by a godlike king.

This unique and complex society came to a sudden, dramatic halt with the arrival of the Spanish conquistadors. With small forces, but great technical superiority, the Spanish dealt a deathblow to the Aztecs by capturing Tenochtitlán in 1521.

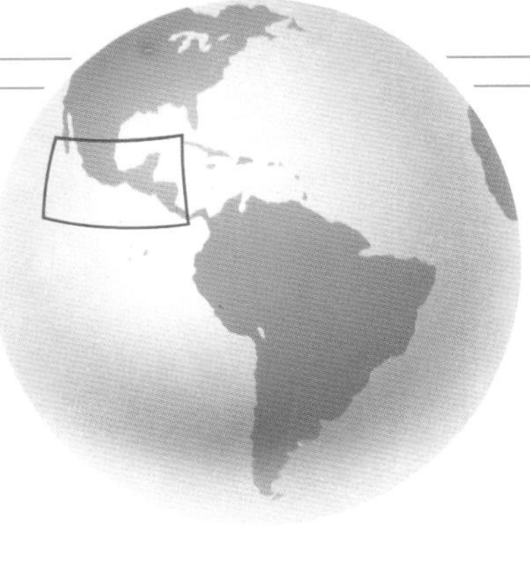

Above The Aztecs inherited much from Mayan and Toltec culture, including aspects of their religion, their scientific achievements, and their calendar. This stone calendar represents the Aztecs' idea of the universe.

Below Tlaloc, the rain god, played an important role in the Aztec religion, for the success of the crops depended on him. This stone sculpture shows the forceful scale and bold, rectangular shapes found in much of Aztec art.

A thirst for blood

Most of the Meso-American cultures appear to have practiced human sacrifice to the gods who protected them. The Aztecs took this tradition to an even greater extreme, and an estimated 20,000 victims were sacrificed by them every year. The sacrifice was performed by priests at altars on the top of the stepped pyramids. They used sharp stone knives made of obsidian or chalcedony to kill the victim and then to gouge out the heart. This practice provided the Spanish conquistadors with a convenient excuse to eradicate the pagan Aztec culture in the name of Christianity.

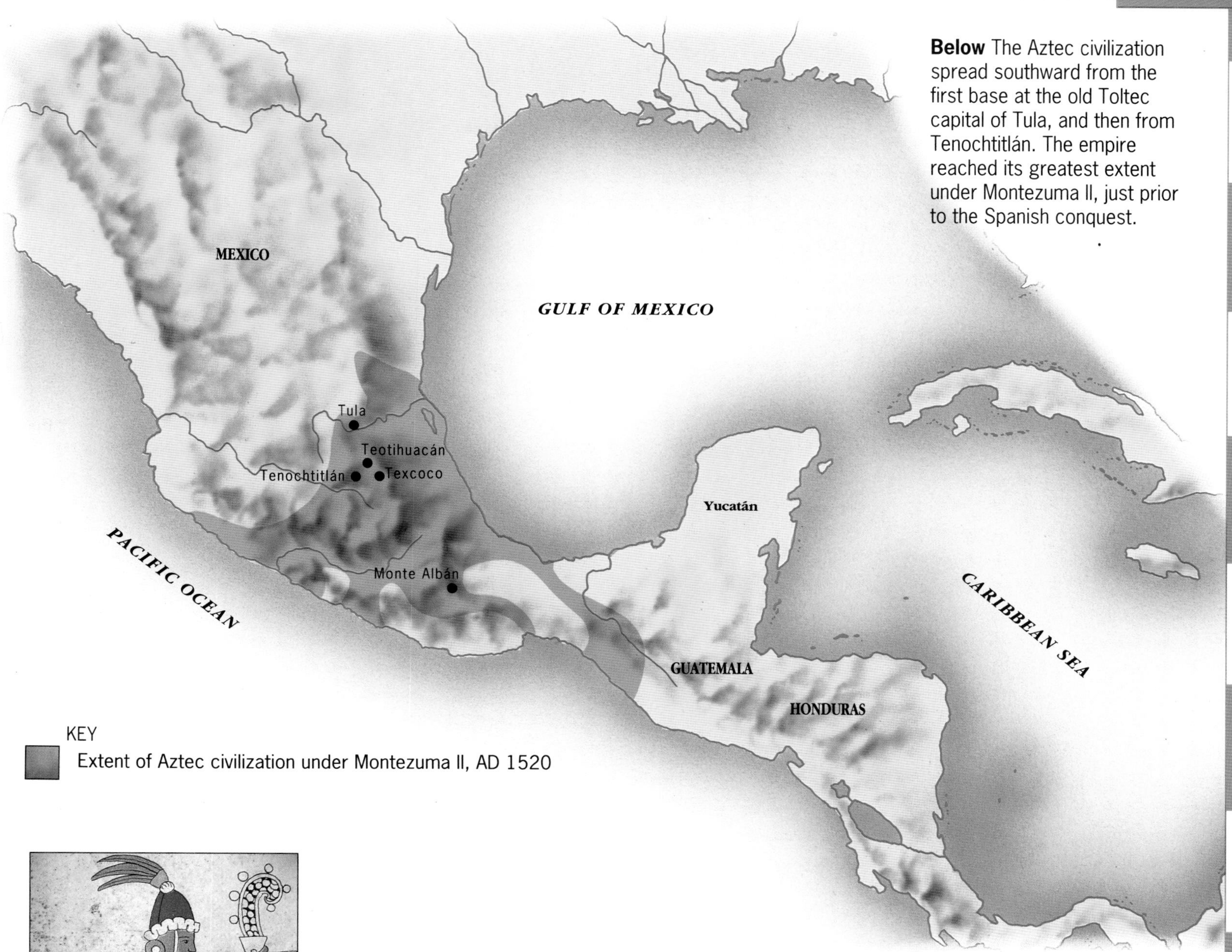

Below The Aztec civilization spread southward from the first base at the old Toltec capital of Tula, and then from Tenochtitlán. The empire reached its greatest extent under Montezuma II, just prior to the Spanish conquest.

MEXICO
GULF OF MEXICO
Tula
Teotihuacán
Tenochtitlán
Texcoco
Yucatán
PACIFIC OCEAN
Monte Albán
CARIBBEAN SEA
GUATEMALA
HONDURAS

KEY
Extent of Aztec civilization under Montezuma II, AD 1520

Above This picture from an Aztec-style codex shows Quetzalcoatl, the Toltec feathered-serpent god adopted by the Aztecs. The Aztecs had numerous deities. The national god was Huitzilopochtli (the hummingbird); the serpent-skirted Coatlicue was his mother and an earth goddess; the goddess of love was Tlazolteotl. Other gods were introduced from the conquered territories of their empire. The deities had their own temples and each demanded a share of human sacrifice.

Spanish conquest

After Columbus reached the Caribbean in 1492, the Spanish quickly established a foothold in Cuba and other islands. From there they continued their conquest in search of gold and territory and converts to Christianity.

Hernán Cortés (1485-1547) landed in Yucatán in 1519, at the head of a company of just 600 men. These numbers swelled rapidly, as he was able to make alliances with local peoples who had no affection for their Aztec rulers. Cortés also had gunpowder, armor and horses, none of which the Aztecs had seen before.

Cortés and his allies marched on Tenochtitlán. The Aztecs welcomed them, but treated them warily. Cortés then took as hostage the great Aztec emperor Montezuma II (reigned 1502-1520), who had been discouraged by various ominous omens. After Montezuma was killed, reputedly by the Aztecs themselves, the Spanish then laid siege to Tenochtitlán, which fell in 1521. Within five years Cortés had conquered all the Aztec territories. Disease and warfare then brought a rapid end to the Aztec civilization.

THE INCAS

While civilization was evolving in Meso-America (see pages 80-83), developments were also taking place in the western Andes. The starting point was the cultivation of corn around 2500 BC, later supplemented by potatoes. The first major temple-city was built at Tiahuanaco some time before AD 500. In the 6th century AD a number of warlike states emerged, such as the Moche and Nazca, who were noted also for their pottery and textiles.

Lost world

The Spanish had conquered most of the Inca Empire by 1539, but they never found the city of Machu Picchu, perched high in the Andes above Cuzco. It was discovered by the American archaeologist Hiram Bingham in 1911. It seems likely that some Incas withdrew to this city after the Spanish had conquered Cuzco, but just when it was abandoned, or why, remains a mystery.

The Incas had no metal tools capable of cutting stone. Instead they shaped it with hammers made of even harder stone, such as quartzite. At Machu Picchu the size of the stones is relatively modest. Elsewhere, as at Cuzco for instance, they are vast. They were cut to irregular shapes, but then fitted together with such precision that they needed no mortar. Some of the stones weigh 100 tons. Since the Incas did not have the wheel, no one knows how the stones were taken from the quarries to the site itself.

Below Gold was readily available to the Andean cultures. It was used to make tools, such as needles and fish-hooks, as well as jewelry and ornaments. This Chimu cat's head shows the imagination that goldworkers applied to their craft.

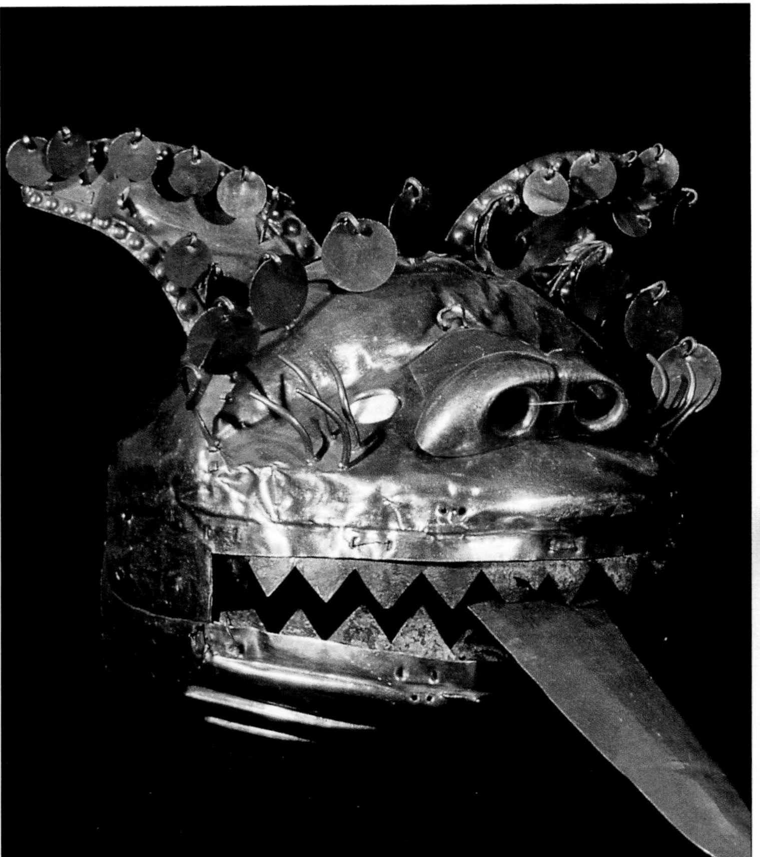

In the 9th century the Huari in Peru established military power over their neighbors. They were succeeded in the 14th and 15th centuries by the Chimu. The Incas were latecomers, expanding their empire after 1440.

The Inca emperor ruled from the capital at Cuzco with the absolute authority of a god. Society was strictly ordered and controlled by appointed government officials. A network of roads spanned the empire. All land was owned by the emperor, but state funds were used for the welfare of the aged and the sick. The Inca religion involved sacrifice—usually of animals but sometimes of humans.

Because the Incas did not develop a writing system, information about them has been pieced together from artifacts and archaeological finds. And records were kept by chroniclers accompanying the Spanish, who destroyed the Incas swiftly after 1532.

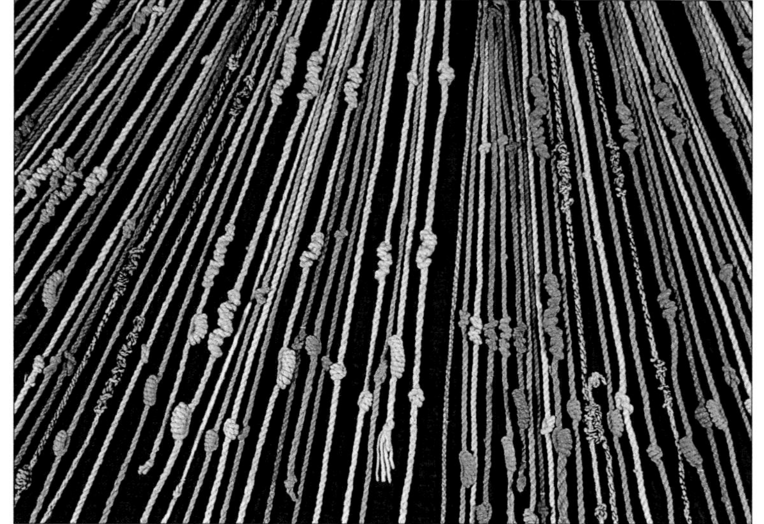

Above The Incas developed a system of counting using hanks of colored strings and knots. These *quipus* were used to keep records, and were also a convenient way to send secret messages.

Right The Andean peoples were gifted sculptors, working in gold, pottery, and wood. This wooden Nazca figure wears a typical costume of a noble: loincloth, turban, and large disc-shaped earplugs.

The lure of gold

Francisco Pizarro (about 1470-1541) destroyed the Inca Empire with a tiny force of 185 men in 1532. He exploited a squabble between two princes, Huascar and Atahualpa, over succession to the throne. Capturing Atahualpa by trickery, he took delivery of a ransom in gold, but killed Atahualpa anyway. The Spanish, portrayed with Incas on this pot from the 17th century, became the new masters.

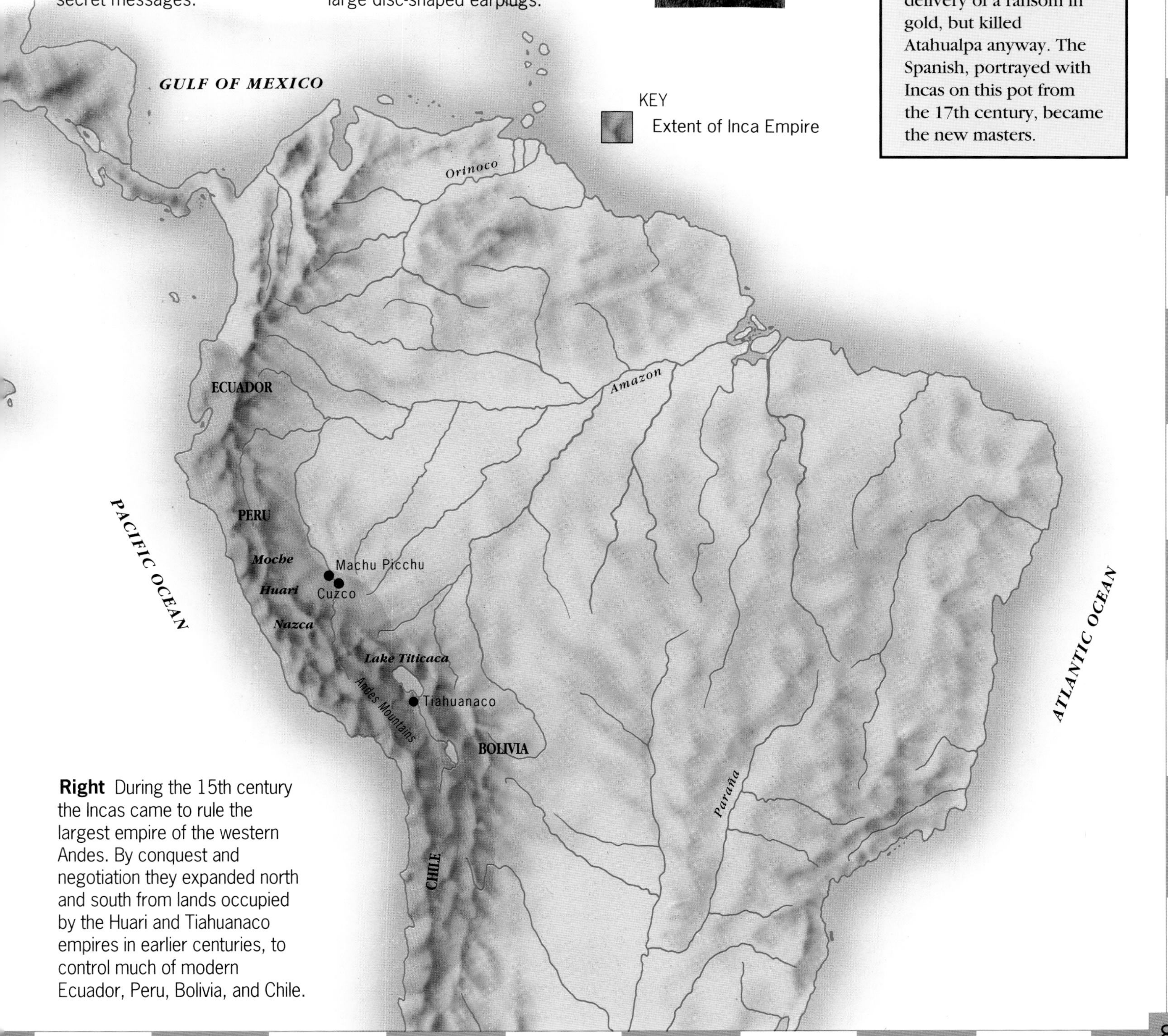

KEY
Extent of Inca Empire
GULF OF MEXICO
Orinoco
Amazon
ECUADOR
PERU
PACIFIC OCEAN
Moche
Huari
Nazca
Machu Picchu
Cuzco
Lake Titicaca
Andes Mountains
Tiahuanaco
BOLIVIA
CHILE
Paraña
ATLANTIC OCEAN

Right During the 15th century the Incas came to rule the largest empire of the western Andes. By conquest and negotiation they expanded north and south from lands occupied by the Huari and Tiahuanaco empires in earlier centuries, to control much of modern Ecuador, Peru, Bolivia, and Chile.

SECTION 9: AFRICA

Africa was probably the birthplace of human life, and also the site of one of the first great civilizations, ancient Egypt. The societies which evolved south of the Sahara developed a highly distinctive cultural heritage, but they were not city-builders.

EARLY AFRICAN KINGDOMS

Africa has two separate, but linked, channels of history. The story of ancient Egypt and the rest of North Africa is linked to that of the Mediterranean and West Asia. But Egyptian civilization strongly influenced the kingdom of Kush in Nubia to its south. From Nubia a way of life revolving around crop-raising and herding spread across the southern Sahara to West Africa, where the iron-smelting Nok culture arose about the 3rd century BC. After AD 100 Negro Bantu farmers and iron-smelters migrated east and south into areas traditionally inhabited by hunter-gatherers.

Several mighty kingdoms rose up in West Africa, which became rich through trade in gold, ivory, and slaves, mainly with Berbers and Arabs. The empire of Ghana (8th-12th centuries) was followed by that of Mali (13th-14th centuries), then Songhai (15th-16th centuries). Arab traders also brought Islam to the east coast of Africa after the 9th century, and to West Africa after the 11th century. Mali was an Islamic empire, and so too was Songhai.

The Europeans first arrived on the West African coast in the 15th century. This led to great changes in coastal Africa, but the interior was only directly affected after the period of rapid European colonization toward the end of the 19th century.

Left After the 1st century BC, settled farming in West Africa established a pattern of life that still continues today in rural areas. In the agricultural villages, useful and decorative objects were produced from readily available materials. Any crop surpluses were traded at the local market.

Timbuktu

Gold was found in parts of West Africa around the Niger River. Timbuktu lies close to the river, and is also at the end of the old caravan routes that crossed the Sahara. It became the capital of the Mali Empire in the 14th century, and was famous for its great wealth. Timbuktu fascinated the Europeans, but by the time the first explorer reached the city, in 1827, it had declined and long since lost its wealth.

Below The craftsmen of Benin—a region in the south of modern Nigeria—were famous for their bronze casting. This plaque portrays an *oba*, or ruler, as a divine being. His fish-like feet are the symbol of the sea-god Olokun. Benin became wealthy after the arrival of the Europeans in the 15th century. The coastal traders exchanged slaves, gold, and ivory for textiles, tools, and guns.

Left Most African buildings were made from the best material available locally—mud-brick. Great Zimbabwe is a rare exception. This large complex, with a palace and fortifications, is built in stone. It dates from the 14th and 15th centuries, when its rulers controlled the valuable gold trade with Arabs on the coast. The pattern of life there was probably very similar to that in other African royal villages.

Below Early cultural changes in Africa generally took place from north to south, first out of Egypt and then out of West Africa. Most of the modern map of Africa is based on the boundaries established by European colonial rule in the late 19th century.

MEDITERRANEAN SEA
Atlas Mountains
Sahara Desert
NUBIA
Nile
RED SEA
Timbuktu
Niger
Congo
Mombasa
Kilwa
Zambezi
Limpopo
Kalahari Desert
Orange
MADAGASCAR
SOUTH ATLANTIC

KEY
Empire of Ghana, 8th to 12th centuries
Empire of Mali, 13th to 14th centuries
Empire of Songhai, 15th to 16th centuries
Empire of Zimbabwe, 14th to 15th centuries
Nok culture
Benin culture

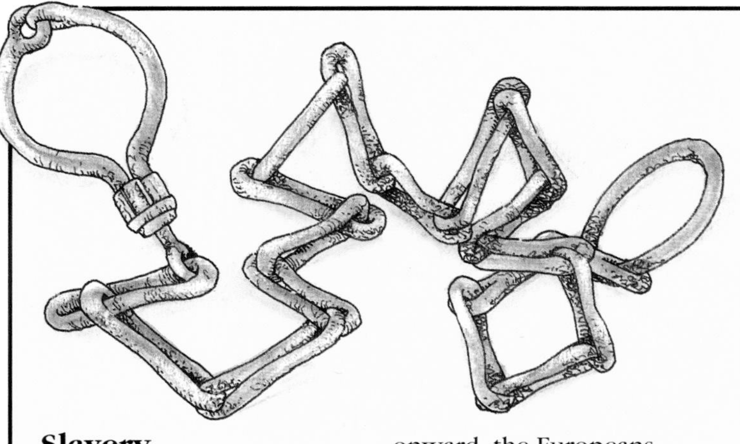

Slavery

The Europeans did not invent slavery, which was widely practiced in the ancient world. The Arabs had been slave-trading in Africa for centuries. From the late 16th century onward, the Europeans removed 10 million slaves from Africa, mainly to work in new plantations in the Americas, often in conditions of exceptional cruelty. This was devastating to African civilization.

SECTION 10: AUSTRALASIA AND OCEANIA

From the earliest migrations 50,000 years ago, the distinct cultures of this region have been shaped by the huge variety in climate, by isolation, and by daring exploration. The arrival of Europeans in the 17th century heralded a period of rapid change and conflict.

AUSTRALIAN ABORIGINAL CULTURE

From about 50,000 BC Australia has been inhabited. In the last Ice Age, it was possible to reach Australia from Southeast Asia by a series of land bridges and short passages across water. Around 15,000 years ago the ice caps began to melt and the sea level rose, isolating the Stone Age Aboriginal culture until recent times.

Aboriginal culture was very diverse, strongly influenced by the harsh landscape and climate. The people lived in bands of 20 to 50, and formed loosely connected tribes with other bands. There were as many as 600 of these tribal groups and 300 languages. Some groups lived by fishing and hunting along the fertile coasts, and others inhabited the unforgiving interior. They survived by their finely tuned hunting skills and moved with the seasons across a wide area. Evidence has been found of long-distance trading in quartzite, shells, ochre, axeheads, and boomerangs. No tribal group developed agriculture, but some cleared bush lands with fire to encourage certain plants and game.

The Aborigines had their own art forms, dances, ceremonies, and feasts. Their mythology, particularly the mythology of Dreamtime (see box), played a central role. Only some traces of Aboriginal culture have survived. When the British arrived in Australia in large numbers in the early 19th century, the Aborigines were decimated by disease, by the loss of their lands, and by widespread killings.

Didgeridoo

Song and dance is important in Aboriginal culture. Rhythms are produced by clapping, or by playing a large, hollow drone-pipe called a *didgeridoo.*

Dreamtime

Most Aboriginal artifacts were made of materials that eventually decay. Rock art is one of the few surviving relics of their ancient culture. For this, they used natural pigments, such as charcoal, clay, and dust from ants' nests. Subjects were usually Aboriginal mythology and Dreamtime—the creation myth that explains the origin of the Earth and the animals, and their relationship to human beings. This rock painting (above) is in Arnhem Land, where artists developed an "X-ray" style of painting, showing the bones and internal organs as well as the bodies of the animals.

Left Ayers Rock—called *Uluru* by the Aborigines—is one of the largest single lumps of rock in the world. It rises steeply from the surrounding plain, and often catches the light in a spectacular way, particularly at sunset. Although now a popular tourist attraction, it was always a sacred site of the Aborigines, who knew that it marked the centerpoint of the continent. *Uluru* was restored to Aboriginal ownership in 1985.

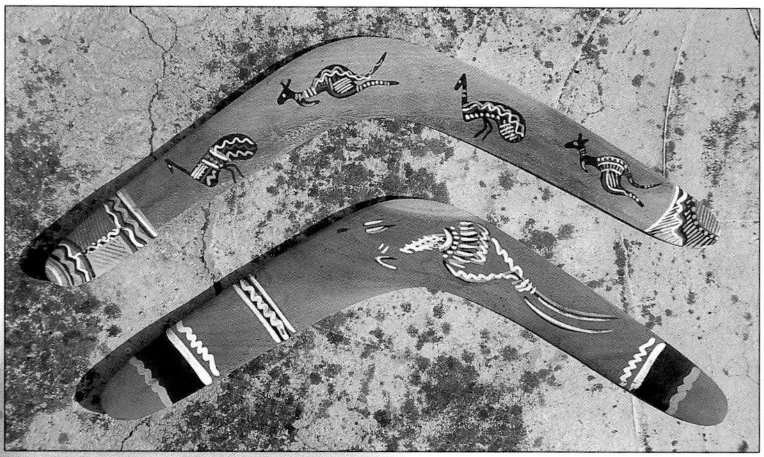

Above The boomerang is the most famous Aboriginal weapon. The lightweight returning boomerang, which flies back to the skilled thrower, was used to play games, or to frighten animals into a trap. But there were much larger versions, up to 6 feet (1.8 m) long, which could be either thrown or used as clubs. The boomerang was used as a weapon in fighting or in stunning prey.

BORNEO
NEW GUINEA
PACIFIC OCEAN
INDIAN OCEAN
TIMOR SEA
CORAL SEA
AUSTRALIA
Ayers Rock
Brisbane 1824
Fremantle 1829
Sydney 1788
Adelaide 1836
Melbourne 1835
TASMANIA

Above Body painting was part of rituals and ceremonies and was often elaborate as well as striking. Aborigines in the hottest parts of Australia wore little or no clothing, but decorated their bodies with necklaces, belts, and armbands.

KEY
Area of dry land during the Ice Age
Dates when cities were founded are shown.

Left Up to about 10,000 BC Australia was attached to New Guinea and Tasmania, forming a vast landmass. Much of the continent is bush and desert, but the Aborigines traversed it. Until the 1860s, the Aborigines were the only people who knew the interior of Australia.

THE PACIFIC ISLANDS AND NEW ZEALAND

The complex map of Oceania is usually divided into three main groups of islands which, over many thousands of years, were gradually inhabited by different peoples.

Melanesia ("black islands") was first inhabited about 10,000 years ago by people who spread out from New Guinea, where they had developed a settled culture and the cultivation of yams and taro. They reached the New Hebrides by about 2000 BC.

Micronesia ("small islands") was first settled in about 3000 BC by people from Southeast Asia. They arrived in Fiji by 1500 BC, and in Tonga and Samoa between 1000 and 500 BC. From here they went on to Polynesia ("many islands")—the group farthest from any mainland—and spread out through the islands with increasingly daring feats of seamanship.

Polynesian settlers reached Hawaii about AD 100, French Polynesia in AD 300, and Easter Island in AD 400. In each of these they developed their culture based on hereditary chiefs and a closely structured social life.

After about AD 950 Polynesians known as Maoris settled in New Zealand. At first they hunted flightless birds (New Zealand had virtually no mammals), but later they farmed sweet potatoes and other root crops. A more aggressive culture developed after 1500, and this spirit fueled Maori resistance to European settlement after the 1840s. The resulting Maori Wars ended in 1871. In the meantime, the Polynesian islands had little defense against the superior might of the European navies, and they too became European colonies.

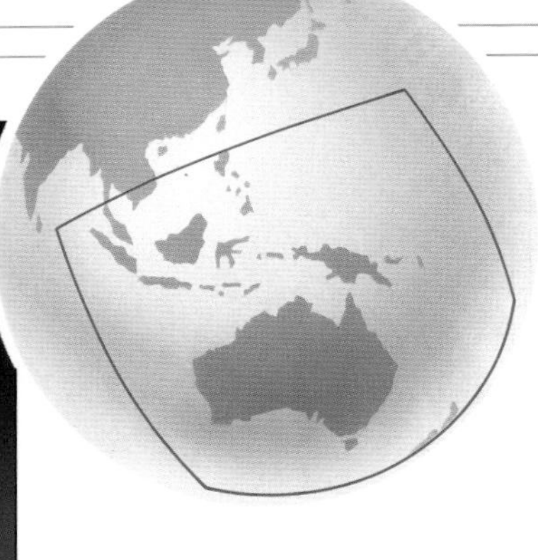

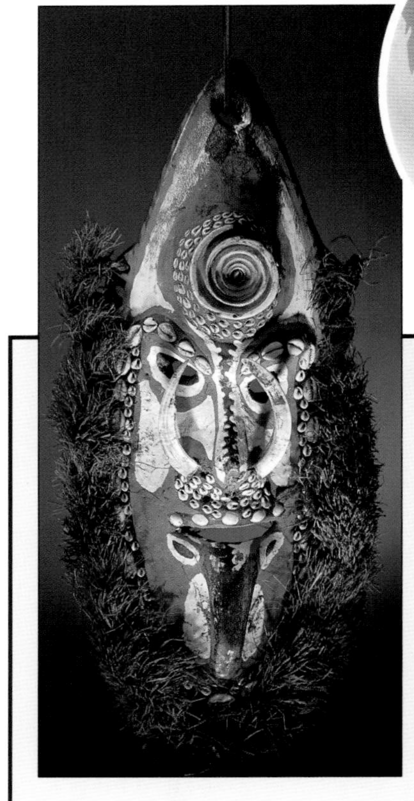

New Stone Age

Until this century, many of the peoples in the remote valleys and highlands of New Guinea lived in a New Stone Age culture in which rituals, ceremonies, and dancing were a central feature. This spectacular mask is decorated with cowrie shells and boar's tusks.

Left The people of the Pacific islands were among the world's most gifted sailors and navigators. Then, as now, they were able to travel for days without sight of land, guided only by the stars, the flight of birds, the shapes of the clouds, and a feel for the swell of the ocean. Double-hulled "outrigger" sailing boats—some of considerable size—were used for journeys between the islands. In New Zealand, the Maoris used sleek and powerful war canoes that were ornately decorated with carved wood. Designed as raiding boats, they were driven by the paddles of 50 or more warriors, and made lightning attacks on the fortified Maori villages that grew up along the coasts after the 1500s.

Above The Polynesians on Easter Island created a cult which remains a mystery to this day. Between AD 1000 and 1600 over 600 huge stone heads were carved and erected on the island, some of them over 40 feet (12 m) tall and weighing 50 tons. Then, suddenly, the cult was abandoned.

Above The Maoris trace their ancestry back to the first settlers who left the Cook Islands for New Zealand about AD 950. Maori nobles had their faces tattooed in spiraling patterns. The technique of tattooing (and the word itself) came from Polynesia.

Below The Maori *tiki* is a good-luck charm and represents the figure of an ancestor. In the Polynesian religion powerful deities were always at war with one another. Respect for them was shown by *taboo*, a system of behavior and ritual that clearly established what was not permitted.

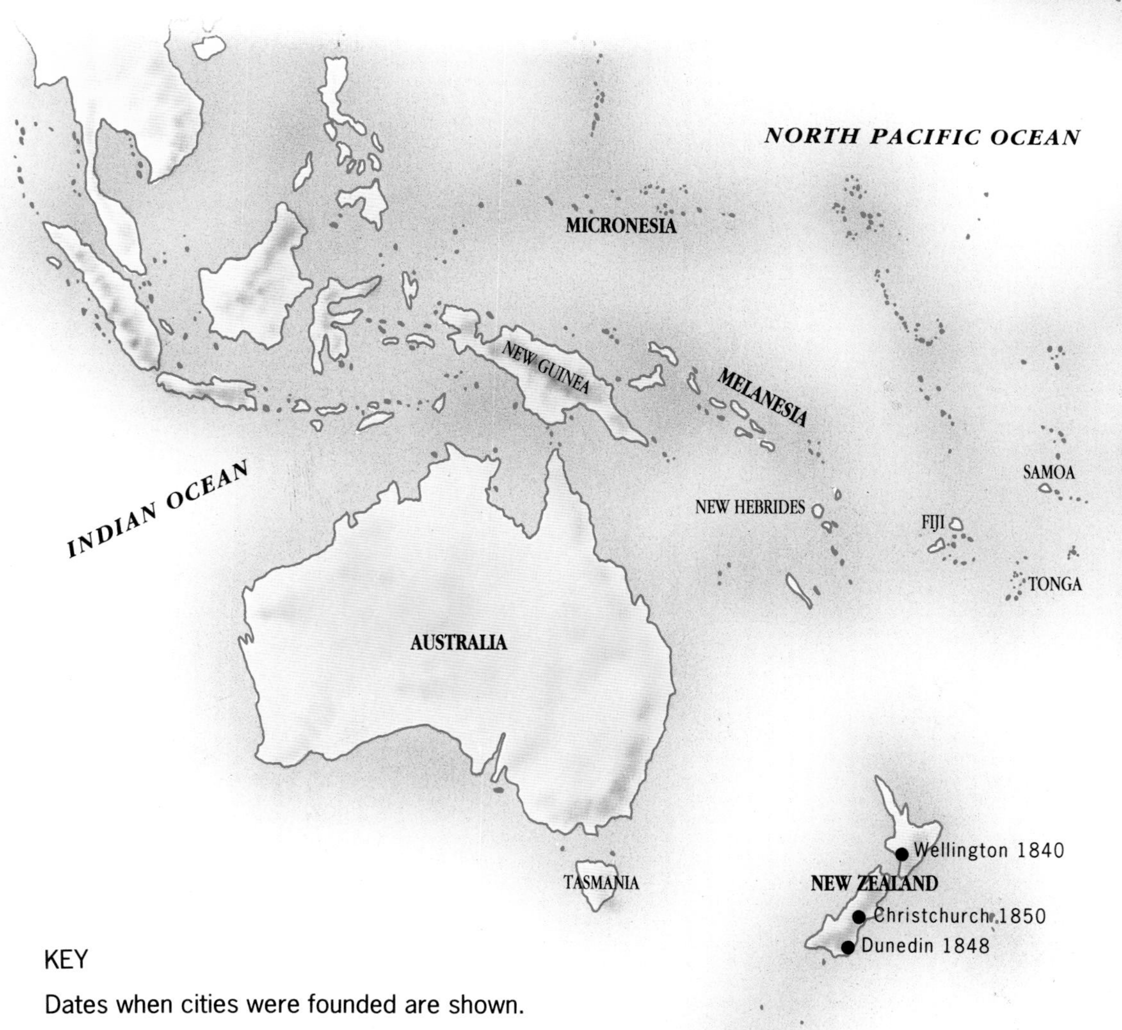

Above The Pacific islands are a sprinkling of tiny landmasses in a vast area of ocean. The settlement of these islands, and the trade carried out between them, depended on the remarkable seamanship of the islanders. The size of the islands of New Zealand, and their temperate climate, explain the distinctive Maori culture that developed there.

TIME CHART

This chart will enable you to trace the rise and fall of civilizations at a glance. The colors of the bars correspond to those in the key on the right. To follow the progress of an individual civilization or region, find it on the left of the chart. Then track it through the centuries marked along the top. The peak of the civilization occurred where the color is deepest.

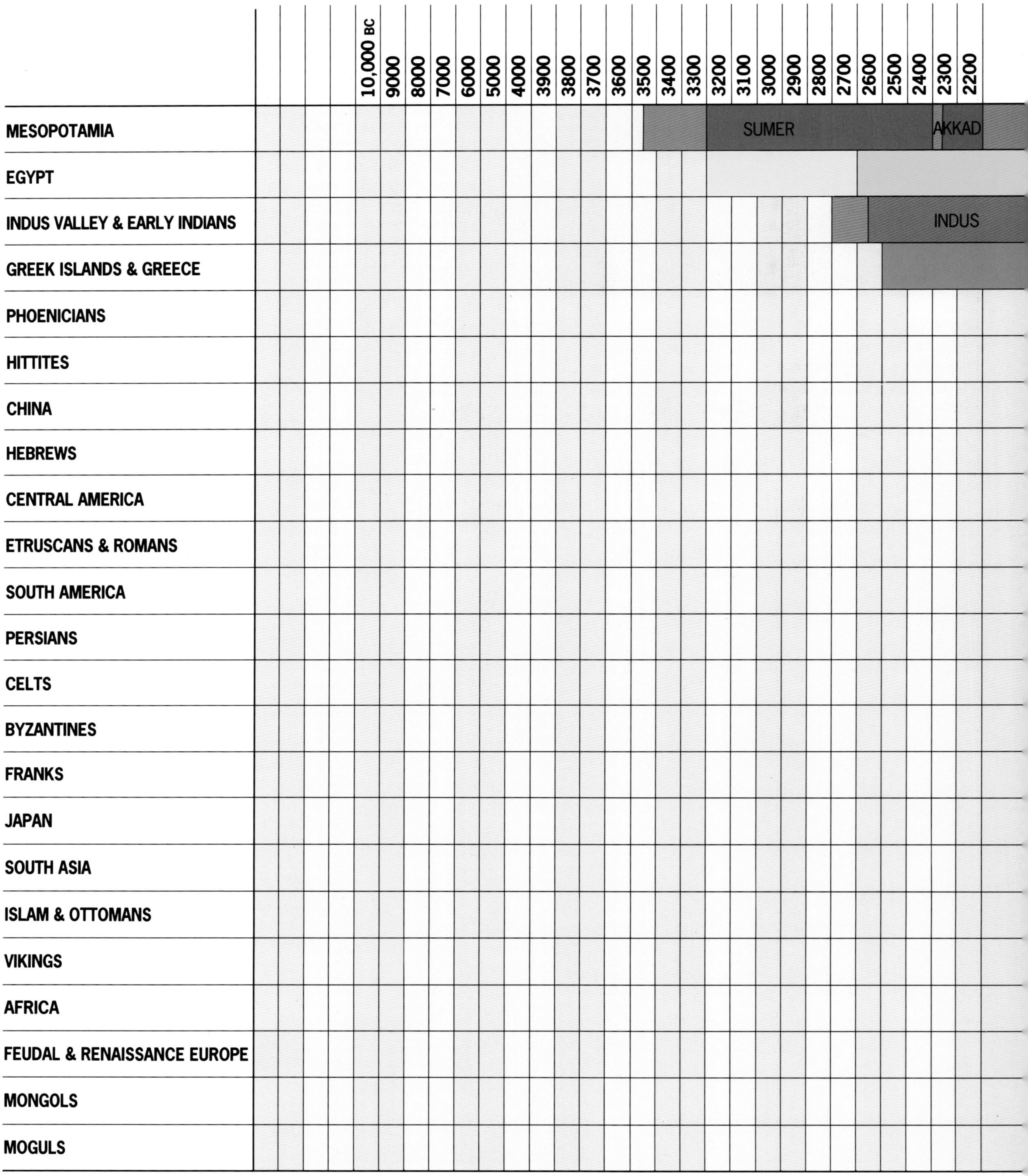

	10,000 BC	9000	8000	7000	6000	5000	4000	3900	3800	3700	3600	3500	3400	3300	3200	3100	3000	2900	2800	2700	2600	2500	2400	2300	2200
MESOPOTAMIA																	SUMER							AKKAD	
EGYPT																									
INDUS VALLEY & EARLY INDIANS																								INDUS	
GREEK ISLANDS & GREECE																									
PHOENICIANS																									
HITTITES																									
CHINA																									
HEBREWS																									
CENTRAL AMERICA																									
ETRUSCANS & ROMANS																									
SOUTH AMERICA																									
PERSIANS																									
CELTS																									
BYZANTINES																									
FRANKS																									
JAPAN																									
SOUTH ASIA																									
ISLAM & OTTOMANS																									
VIKINGS																									
AFRICA																									
FEUDAL & RENAISSANCE EUROPE																									
MONGOLS																									
MOGULS																									

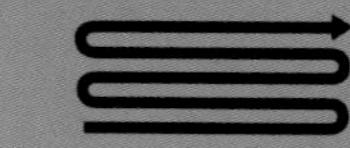

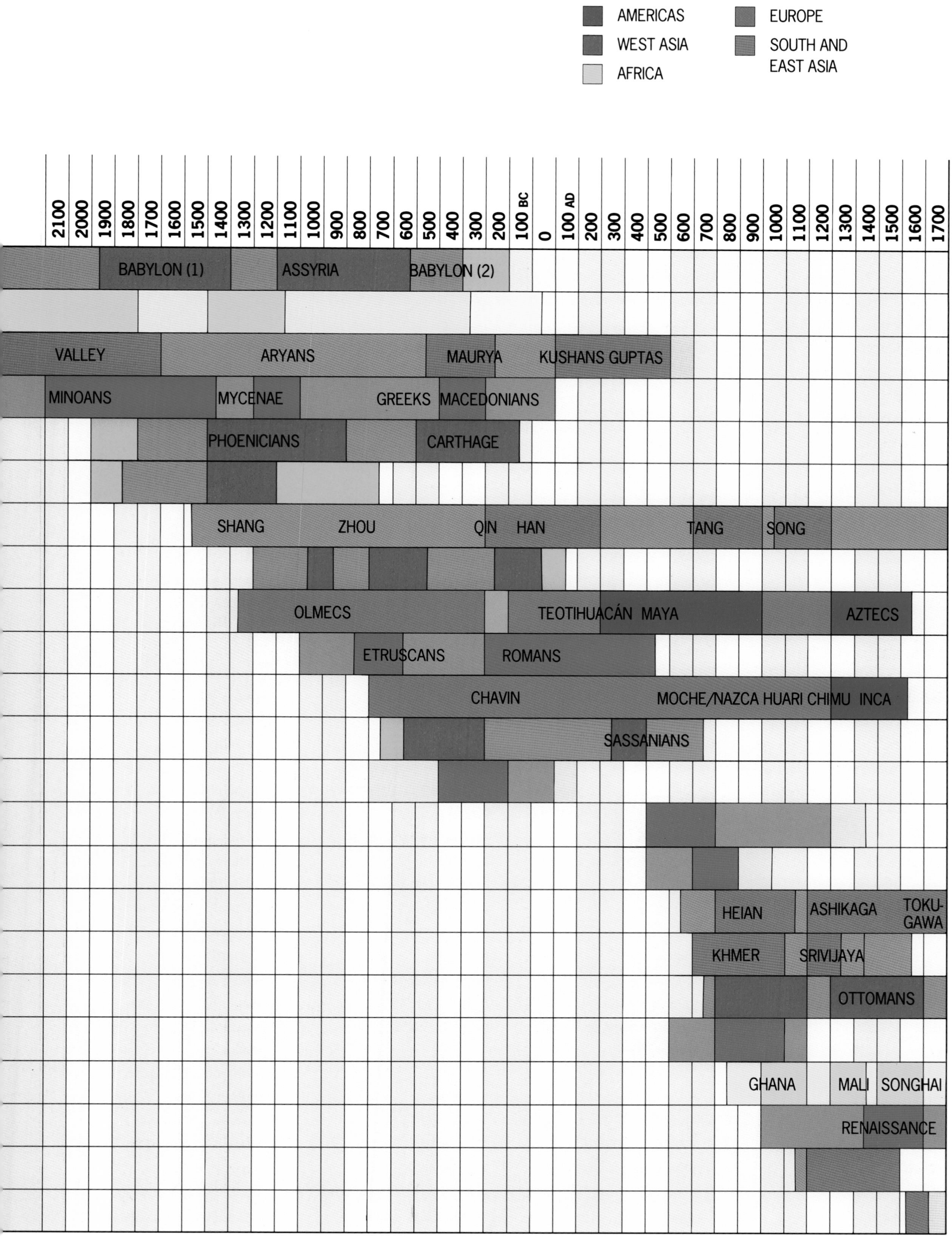

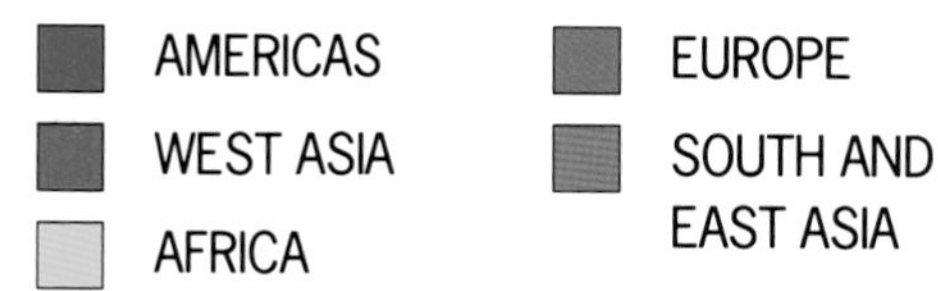

AMERICAS
WEST ASIA
AFRICA
EUROPE
SOUTH AND EAST ASIA
2100
2000
1900
1800
1700
1600
1500
1400
1300
1200
1100
1000
900
800
700
600
500
400
300
200
100 BC
0
100 AD
200
300
400
500
600
700
800
900
1000
1100
1200
1300
1400
1500
1600
1700
BABYLON (1)
ASSYRIA
BABYLON (2)
VALLEY
ARYANS
MAURYA
KUSHANS GUPTAS
MINOANS
MYCENAE
GREEKS
MACEDONIANS
PHOENICIANS
CARTHAGE
SHANG
ZHOU
QIN
HAN
TANG
SONG
OLMECS
TEOTIHUACÁN
MAYA
AZTECS
ETRUSCANS
ROMANS
CHAVIN
MOCHE/NAZCA HUARI CHIMU
INCA
SASSANIANS
HEIAN
ASHIKAGA
TOKU-GAWA
KHMER
SRIVIJAYA
OTTOMANS
GHANA
MALI
SONGHAI
RENAISSANCE

INDEX

ACKNOWLEDGMENTS

Quarto would like to thank the following for providing photographs, and for granting permission to reproduce copyright material:

Lesley and Roy Adkins:TRIP: 60cl; Joan Batten:TRIP: 62cr, 67ac, 72cr; C.C.:TRIP: 66bl; Andoni Canela:TRIP: 87ac; R Cracknell:TRIP: 35al, 48ac, 63c, 63br: Anthony R Dalton/TRIP: 30bl, 31ar, 86br; C M Dixon: 7al, 8ar, 9bl, 11al, 11cl, 11bc, 12br, 13ar, 13bl, 14ar, 14bl, 15ar, 15cl, 16b, 17al, 17bl, 19al, 19cr, 21ar, 21c, 21cr, 25cl, 25bl, 27ac, 27cl, 28ar, 29cr, 30ac, 30ar, 36cr, 38cr, 38bl, 39al, 39cr, 39cl, 40ac, 40cr, 40br, 41ar, 41cr, 42ar, 44ac, 44br, 46cl, 46bc, 47al, 49ar, 49cl, 49br, 50bl, 50br, 51cl, 51cr, 52cr, 52bl, 54ac, 55al, 56ac, 57bl, 57bc, 58ar, 58cr, 58bl, 59ar, 72bl, 76cr, 78br, 79ar, 85ar, 87cl, 91cr; ET Archive: 6cr, 8bl, 9al, 12cl, 14cr, 17cl, 18cr, 20cr, 22cr, 22bl, 23c, 23cr, 24ar, 25br, 31c, 32cr, 33br, 34bl, 35ar, 37br, 42bl, 43bc, 43br, 44cr, 45ar, 46ac, 50ac, 53al, 53cr, 54cr, 54bl, 59al, 60cr, 60bl, 61cl, 61bl, 61br, 68cr, 69al, 71al, 71cr, 73ar, 73cl, 74ar, 74bl, 74br, 77al, 77ac, 83cl, 83br, 84ar, 85al, 85ac, 90ac, 91ac; Jon Evans:Life File: 89al; Eye Ubiquitous:TRIP: 9ar, 18br, 47c, 64bl, 65bl, 67cl, 67cr, 69cr, 71cl, 75br, 76bl, 78cl, 81cr, 88br, 89bl; The Fortean Picture Library:TRIP: 9cr, 36al, 37al, 48cr, 79al, 80ac, 80cr, 81al, 82cr, 91al; Juliet Highet:Life File: 84cl; S Kay:Life File: 31al; Mo Khan:Life File: 16cr; Emma Lee:Life File: 89cl; Mansell Collection: 52ac, 55bc; Antony Mason: 66cr, 76ar; K.N.:TRIP: 86ac; C Parker:TRIP: 81bl; Mike Potter:TRIP: 47cr; Richard Powers:TRIP: 80bl; Quarto: 26ac; P Rauter:TRIP: 73cr; Paul Richards:Life File: 6bl; Helene Rogers:TRIP: 19ar, 33bl, 62cl, 63cl, 64ac, 64cr, 68bl, 69ac, 72ac; Reg Seale:TRIP: 28bl; David Simson:das PHOTO: 56bl, 57br; Jamie Simson:das PHOTO: 29a; Smithsonian Institution, National Archives: 79br; G Spenceley:TRIP: 56br; Roy Styles:TRIP: 45cr; Tokyo National Museum:Life File: 77c; Travel Ink Photo & Feature Library: 70bl, 75bl; TRIP: 7ac, 23ac, 26bl, 32ar, 33cl, 34ar, 82ac; Turkish Tourist Board: 24bl; University of Essex:TRIP: 7cr, 13al, 32bl, 82bl; Andrew Ward:Life File: 48cl; Joan Wakelin:TRIP: 90bl; Michael Wood: 21bl.

(a = above, b = below, c = center, l = left, r = right)

While every effort has been made to trace and acknowledge all copyright holders, we would like to apologize should any omissions have been made.